Cambridge Elements

Elements in Construction Grammar
edited by
Thomas Hoffman
Catholic University of Eichstätt-Ingolstadt
Alexander Bergs
Osnabrück University

UNREALIZED ARGUMENTS AND THE GRAMMAR OF CONTEXT

Rui P. Chaves
University of Buffalo

Paul Kay
University of California, Berkeley

Laura A. Michaelis
University of Colorado Boulder

CAMBRIDGE
UNIVERSITY PRESS

Shaftesbury Road, Cambridge CB2 8EA, United Kingdom

One Liberty Plaza, 20th Floor, New York, NY 10006, USA

477 Williamstown Road, Port Melbourne, VIC 3207, Australia

314–321, 3rd Floor, Plot 3, Splendor Forum, Jasola District Centre,
New Delhi – 110025, India

103 Penang Road, #05–06/07, Visioncrest Commercial, Singapore 238467

Cambridge University Press is part of Cambridge University Press & Assessment,
a department of the University of Cambridge.

We share the University's mission to contribute to society through the pursuit of
education, learning and research at the highest international levels of excellence.

www.cambridge.org
Information on this title: www.cambridge.org/9781009663823

DOI: 10.1017/9781009663786

When citing this work, please include a reference to the DOI 10.1017/9781009663786

First published 2025

A catalogue record for this publication is available from the British Library

ISBN 978-1-009-66382-3 Hardback
ISBN 978-1-009-66383-0 Paperback
ISSN 2753-2674 (online)
ISSN 2753-2666 (print)

Additional resources for this publication at www.cambridge.org/EICG_Chaves

Cambridge University Press & Assessment has no responsibility for the persistence
or accuracy of URLs for external or third-party internet websites referred to in this
publication and does not guarantee that any content on such websites is, or will
remain, accurate or appropriate.

For EU product safety concerns, contact us at Calle de José Abascal, 56, 1°, 28003
Madrid, Spain, or email eugpsr@cambridge.org

Unrealized Arguments and the Grammar of Context

Elements in Construction Grammar

DOI: 10.1017/9781009663786
First published online: June 2025

Rui P. Chaves
University of Buffalo

Paul Kay
University of California, Berkeley

Laura A. Michaelis
University of Colorado Boulder

Author for correspondence: Rui P. Chaves, rchaves@buffalo.edu

Abstract: In null instantiation (NI) an optionally unexpressed argument receives either anaphoric or existential interpretation. One cannot accurately predict a predicator's NI potential based either on semantic factors (e.g., Aktionsart class of the verb) or pragmatic factors (e.g., relative discourse prominence of arguments), but NI potential, while highly constrained, is not simply lexical idiosyncrasy. It is instead the product of both lexical and constructional licensing. In the latter case, a construction can endow a verb with NI potential that it would not otherwise have. Using representational tools of sign based construction grammar, this Element offers a lexical treatment of English null instantiation that covers both distinct patterns of construal of null-instantiated arguments and the difference between listeme-based and contextually licensed, thus construction-based, null complementation.

This Element also has a video abstract:
www.cambridge.org/EICG_Chaves_abstract

Keywords: Null instantiation, Optionality, Pragmatics, Constructions, Context

ISBNs: 9781009663823 (HB), 9781009663830 (PB), 9781009663786 (OC)
ISSNs: 2753-2674 (online), 2753-2666 (print)

Contents

An online appendix can be found at
www.cambridge.org/EICG_Chaves

1 Introduction

Null instantiation (NI), illustrated in (1), provides an exception to the general principle that a predicator's array of required semantic dependents determines its valence, or combinatory potential.

(1)   a.   We won ∅ .   (direct object NI)

   b.   Nixon resigned ∅ .   (oblique object NI)

   c.   ∅ Contains alcohol.   (subject NI in labels)

   d.   ∅ Got up, ∅ got out of bed, ∅ dragged a comb across my head. (subject NI in the diary genre)

There are two ways in which such mismatches of semantic and syntactic valence can occur. Either (i) the lexical entry for the predicator – we will here restrict our attention to verbs – specifies that an argument may remain implicit and be interpreted either definitely or indefinitely or (ii) a contextually sensitive lexical rule licenses a derived verb lexeme with such an option from an otherwise identical verb lexeme lacking it.

   Most recent attempts to address the factors that license implicit arguments in English have rejected Fillmore's view of the NI affordance as primarily a matter of lexical stipulation (Fillmore, 1986), instead ascribing the implicit-role option to semantic or usage factors – the latter of which include predictability of the target argument and its importance in context (O'Gorman, 2019). Resnik (1993, 1996) attributes NI potential to the governing verb's selectivity – that is, how predictable an implicit object's type is from that verb lemma. The intuition here is that NI is an instance of "deletion up to recoverability" per the second quantity maxim (Horn, 1984). Transit verbs *board* and *deplane*, which show a high rate of omitted objects, seem to affirm the selectivity effect. At the same time, these verbs have definite (anaphoric) null objects (the aircraft) rather than indefinite ones – a fact that the Resnik model does not seem to predict, as it does not offer clear predictions about the construal of an NI argument.

   In addition, corpus studies like Ruppenhofer (2004, ch. 4) and Heider (2005) show that argument predictability is not a sufficient condition for optionality. Using a larger sample of verbs than Resnik (1993), Heider (2005) shows that the correlation between the syntactic optionality and each verb's selectional strength is significantly diluted by the presence of low-frequency verbs in the the analysis (36 additional direct object verbs that occur at least 50 times in the British National Corpus), with a very small effect size (Cohen's $d = 0.21$), suggesting that differences between obligatory and optional verbs are weaker in larger datasets. Moreover, just as in Resnik (1993), Heider (2005) found no clear sectional strength cut-off point between the obligatory and optional object verbs classes. Indeed, Ruppenhofer (2004) points out that in the absence of a type-frequency threshold above which implicit objects are permitted, Resnik's model makes no specific predictions for NI. The predictability account is also undermined by the existence of verbs which do not license object NI despite having extremely restrictive – and thus presumably predictable – object requirements. For instance, the verb *diagonalize* has only one licit direct-object type (McCawley, 1968, 134), and *devein* has a very restricted set (McCawley, 1968; Ruppenhofer, 2004), and yet neither allows the omission of their otherwise strongly predicted direct object(s) (e.g. *I diagonalized* *(*the matrix*), and *I deveined* *(*the shrimp / pepper / meat / leaf*)). Comparably selective verbs of removal, including *core*, *gut*, *delouse*, and *defrost*, serve to underscore this point: These verbs have very restricted arrays of object arguments but no NI potential – or at least not in the neutral context of an event report – for example, *??I defrosted yesterday* (Ruppenhofer & Michaelis, 2014).

Several corpus analyses offer predictions about argument-omission patterns based on the semantic role or construal of the omitted argument. Using the FrameNet Annotation Database, Ruppenhofer & Michaelis (2014) propose an implicational regularity that predicts a uniform interpretation type (indefinite null instantiation [INI] or definite null instantiation [DNI]) for a given frame element across all lexical units of the frame that allows that frame element's omission. David (2016, 5, 6), who likewise uses FrameNet annotated data, proposes that "the omissible element usually qualifies, at an image-schematic level, as the ground in a figure-ground relation." David observes, for example, that the PP complements in partitive expressions (e.g. those headed by *portion*, *piece*, *flock*) are uniformly omissible. Based on the results of a cross-linguistic corpus study and sentence-completion experiment, Reinöhl & Ellison (2024) claim that metaphorical construal of a functor "forces overtness" of its complement. They observe, for example, that the verb *arrive* welcomes omission of the goal argument in a literal passage like *While we waited in the lobby, Kim arrived* ∅ but not in a metaphoric context – for example, *Although everything had been pointing to this conclusion, Kim only recently arrived* *(*at it*). They demonstrate a consistent effect of metaphoric construal across three corpus studies (Indo-Aryan languages, British English, Vera'a) and a large-scale English sentence-completion experiment. They do not, however, definitely rule out the potential effects of frequency. Together, these studies demonstrate that some argument-realization tendencies are attributable to frame-semantic properties of lexical units and constructions, but all are narrow in scope, demonstrating these effects for just a few frames or a few predicators.

Goldberg (2006, ch. 5) views NI as a form of discourse-conditioned argument omission, postulating that unrealized arguments express "semantic participants" whose type or identity is either (a) irrelevant to the message conveyed by the predication or (b) recoverable from context. But while treating NI largely as a pragmatic effect, Goldberg (2006, ch. 5) also recognizes the influence of linguistic convention: She observes that languages differ with regard to the discourse factors that condition NI and proposes a construction to capture constraints on English NI, the Object Deprofiling construction. Rice (1988, 203) offers a profiling-based account as well. She avers "certain construals of transitive events are such that they focus on the active participant and leave the acted-upon participant unspecified and, most importantly, to be filled in with a default value." Profiling-based accounts capture some aspects of verbs' flexibility in context, but like predictability accounts, do not clearly differentiate between implicit arguments interpreted anaphorically, as mutually identifiable referents (e.g. *She resigned [from the company/there]*), and those interpreted existentially (*She retired [from some company/somewhere]*), nor do they see such differences as the products of linguistic convention: There is no reason in principle that *resign* should have a "recoverable" locative argument and *retire* a "deprofiled" one (Ruppenhofer & Michaelis, 2014). Additionally, profiling-based accounts fail to reckon with the lexical idiosyncrasies that inspired Fillmore's 1986 framework. For example, nearly synonymous verb pairs differentially allow omission of the theme argument, as seen in (2). See Fillmore (1986), Mittwoch (2005), and Gillon (2012) for many other examples.

(2)　a.　He chewed the chunk of meat in his mouth for a moment, and then swallowed/*ingested Ø.

　　b.　One of the doors was left unlocked. I was the first to notice/* discover Ø.

　　c.　When you finish/*complete Ø , come show it to me.

Similarly, a predicate can exhibit different NI behaviors in different languages (Fillmore, 1986; Lambrecht & Lemoine, 2005; Ruppenhofer & Michaelis, 2010). For instance, the Portuguese examples in (3) are not licit in English.

(3)　[Tasting a wine]
　　A: Ø Gosta Ø ?
　　　"Like"
　　　[You] like [it]?

B: Ø Gosto Ø .
 "Like"
 [I] like [it].

Lexical-semantic accounts of NI, most prominently Rappaport Hovav & Levin (1998), have focused on the necessity of the target argument in the logical structure of an event. Rappaport Hovav & Levin (1998) attempt to predict a verb's NI potential from its Aktionsart class. They propose that a verb's argument-realization properties result from the combination of the verb's idiosyncratic lexical information with one of five event-structure templates, each of which corresponds to a generally recognized Aktionsart class. Omissible arguments are those that belong to the verb's semantics but not the event-structure template. Rappaport Hovav and Levin (1998, 115) follow Brisson (1994) in assuming that participants supplied exclusively by verb semantics are subject only to a recoverability condition based on prototypicality, which corresponds to what we call existential (or indefinite) interpretation. Take, for example, *like*, a State verb, and *discuss*, an Activity verb, which are assumed by Rappaport Hovav and Levin (1998) to be lexically bivalent but structurally monovalent. Since each of the State and Activity templates has a single (subject) argument, the sentences in (4) are incorrectly predicted to be acceptable.

(4)　a.　*We like Ø .　　　　　　　　　　　　　　　(State verb)

　　b.　*We discussed Ø .　　　　　　　　　　　　(Activity verb)

Rappaport Hovav and Levin (1998) further claim that Accomplishment verbs do not allow NI. Accomplishment verbs, like transitive *break* and *dry*, are modeled as externally caused change-of-state events, and the object argument is accordingly represented as a structure participant – the single argument of the BECOME operator. As Ruppenhofer and Michaelis (2014) and Goldberg (2006, ch. 9) point out, however, Accomplishment predications that disallow null complements when interpreted episodically allow them in generic-habitual contexts, as in (5) and similar cases originally noted by Rizzi (1986).[1]

(5)　a.　That movie always shocks Ø .
　　　　(Levin, 1993, 38)

　　b.　She impresses Ø every time.
　　　　(Ruppenhofer & Michaelis, 2014)

---

[1] This observation is formalized in Section 3.3 as the dispositional NI construction in (65).

But even outside of habitual contexts, a derived version of such psych-verbs can sometimes still license NI, as shown in (6).[2]

(6)   a. [@]The Grammy winner stunned ∅ in a ruby-colored sequin gown, three weeks after welcoming her second child with husband Offset.

  b. [@]She impressed ∅ in a long train dress with a plunging neckline.

  c. [@]Walking the red carpet before the show, she shocked ∅ in a backless minidress featuring pictures of deceased rappers Biggie Smalls and Tupac.

The foregoing observations establish that a verb's Aktionsart class underdetermines its NI potential. In fact, none of the proposed factors is sufficient to predict the existence of nonconstructional, lexical NI. To our knowledge, no formally explicit account has been proposed that recognizes the lexeme-specific constraints on Definite NI (DNI) and Indefinite NI (INI) noted by Fillmore (1986) or the ability of certain semantic or discourse contexts to overcome lexeme-based prohibitions against NI, as in the many genre-specific NI exceptions pointed out by Ruppenhofer and Michaelis (2010). Thus, even strongly anti-NI verbs like *devour* can allow NI:

(7)   Fire can purify ∅ or devour ∅ . Water can cleanse ∅ or drown ∅ .
    [COCA ACAD 1995]

Past analyses of nonrealization generally make appeal to a single mechanism – for example, meaning postulate (Fodor & Fodor, 1980), lexical rule (Dowty, 1985), a pragmatic rule (Culicover & Jackendoff, 2005; Jackendoff, 1987), or, as noted, a mismatch between semantic-role array of the verb and that of the event-structure template with which the verb combines (Levin & Rappaport Hovav, 2005; Rappaport Hovav & Levin, 1998) – but as Cornish (2007, 189) correctly notes, "[a] satisfactory account of the possibility of non-realisation of one or both of a predicate's internal arguments syntactically, and when this is possible, of the kind of interpretation they may receive, requires recognizing the existence of an interaction amongst lexical-semantic structure, the construction selected as a whole, and various discourse-contextual factors." In our view, one must add lexical idiosyncrasy. Moreover, to our knowledge, no formally explicit account has been proposed that recognizes the lexeme-specific constraints on DNI and INI noted

---

[2] Following Bender and Kathol (2001), we use the symbol "[@]" to indicate that an example is attested online; see Online Appendix for the web address of each. In these uses, the verbs denote something closer to "dazzle" than to their canonical meaning.

by Fillmore (1986) or the ability of certain morphosyntactic and discourse contexts to overcome lexeme-based prohibitions against NI, as in the many genre-specific NI exceptions pointed out by Ruppenhofer & Michaelis (2014).

In brief, NI is licensed by two distinct kinds of linguistic specifications. First, it is licensed by language-specific, idiosyncratic constraints in predicators' lexical entries. Thus, translation-equivalent words in different languages, and near synonyms within a single language, can differ with respect to both their NI potentials and the construal of an implicit argument. Second, there are particular constructions which reflect pragmatic constraints whose effect is to create NI potential in predicators that would not otherwise exhibit it. These include constructions that impose constraints on discourse context, narrative context, and shared background knowledge. In this Element we propose a lexical treatment of null instantiation that accounts for: (a) the difference between null complementation licensed by lexical entries, or, equivalently, listemes (i.e. individual "off-the-shelf" lexical entries) as against contextual factors; (b) distinct patterns of construal, whereby certain null-instantiated arguments are interpreted as having definite anaphoric reference and others as having indefinite reference. Section 2 provides an empirical overview of the types of implicit argument phenomena that we focus on, and Section 3 presents a formally explicit theory of the grammar of English implicit arguments, including their interpretation. We employ Sign-Based Construction Grammar (SBCG; Michaelis 2012; Sag 2012), a version of Head-Driven Phrase Structure Grammar (HPSG) that draws from earlier work in Berkeley Construction Grammar (Fillmore, 1988, 2013; Kay, 2002; Kay & Fillmore, 1999), which is ideally suited to characterizing lexical and phrasal generalizations with varying degrees of idiosyncrasy in their syntactic, semantic, and pragmatic interactions.

2 Null Instantiation

Fillmore (1969, 1986), Shopen (1973), and other scholars have noted two distinct kinds of NI of arguments: INI and DNI. Indefinite null instantiation may be viewed in the first instance as a kind of lexically constrained convention of existential import. If I say, "I have contributed to the Red Cross," I have said enough to indicate that I contributed *something*, usually a sum of money or goods of some kind, to the Red Cross. I don't have to mention the stuff of any contribution. In effect I have said that there is some stuff x such that I have contributed x to the Red Cross. On the other hand, if I say, "I contributed \$25," my utterance is only felicitous in a context in which I can take for granted that my addressee can identify the entity to which I made the contribution. The latter example illustrates DNI. This distinction explains why INI has a universal reading in negative sentences, whereas DNI does not, as noted by Condoravdi & Gawron (1996, 3):

(8)　a.　I didn't contribute Ø to the Red Cross.　　　　(Ø = "anything")

　　b.　I didn't contribute $25 Ø .　　　　(Ø = "to it")

Fillmore emphasizes the lexical idiosyncrasy of null complementation, writing:

> It is possible to find closely synonymous words, some of which permit definite null complements while others do not. To mention just one example, we can see that INSIST allows its complement to be absent under the relevant conditions, but many of its near-synonyms do not. Thus, a possible reply to WHY DID YOU MARRY HER? might be **(10)**, but not **(11)** or **(12)** [Boldface example numbers are those of the original].

> 　**(10)**　BECAUSE MOTHER INSISTED
> 　**(11)**　*BECAUSE MOTHER REQUIRED
> 　**(12)**　*BECAUSE MOTHER DEMANDED (Fillmore, 1986, 98)

Fillmore (1986, 99) gives an additional dozen or so examples of fairly close synonyms that display conflicting null complementation potentials. However, as Fillmore also notes, semantics is not uniformly uncorrelated with null complement potential. For example, the verb *give* has the null complement potential of *contribute* only when it is employed with the sense of *contribute*. Thus, one can say **(13a)** but not **(13b)**.

　　(13)　a.　I gave to my NPR station this year.
　　　　　b.　*I gave to my niece on her birthday.

Additional examples of lexical semantic idiosyncrasy of NI include syntactically related *bring* in the sense of "donate," *bequeath*, and *bestow*. *Bring* shares with *contribute* the potential of DNI for the recipient argument but not the INI potential for the theme argument. *Bequeath* and *bestow* share neither of these NI possibilities, as illustrated in (9).

(9)　a.　I will bring a salad to the picnic.

　　b.　*I will bring _[something] to the picnic.

　　c.　I will bring a salad _[to you know what].

　　d.　*I will bring _[something] _[to you know what].

　　e.　I will bequeath *Ø　*Ø .

　　f.　I will bestow *Ø　*Ø .

None of the accounts surveyed in Section 1 recognizes the existence of DNI. Moreover, to our knowledge, no formally explicit account has been proposed that recognizes the lexeme-specific constraints on DNI and INI noted by Fillmore (1986) or the ability of certain morphosyntactic and discourse contexts to overcome lexeme-based prohibitions against NI, as in the many genre-specific NI exceptions pointed out by Ruppenhofer and Michaelis (2014). To capture such contextual overrides, and how NI phenomena interact with the overall grammar, we will propose that NI may be licensed by a lexical entry or by a derivational construction. In the latter case, we suggest, the construction endows a verb with an NI potential that it would not otherwise have.

Fillmore (1986) is concerned exclusively with null complementation that is licensed by particular listemes (i.e. individual "off-the-shelf" lexical entries). We consider this aspect of the phenomenon first, in Section 2.1. Null complementation that is licensed by certain aspects of discourse context is considered in Section 2.2. Other types of implicit argument are discussed in Section 2.3.

2.1 Lexically Licensed NI

Usually or always, lexically licensed NI occurs as an alternative to overt instantiation.[3] Consider the English verb *contribute*. Since the object is optionally INI and the PP complement is optionally DNI, one has paradigmatic examples like (10).[4]

(10)   a.   I will contribute ten dollars to your campaign.

     b.   I will contribute _[something] to your campaign.

     c.   I will contribute ten dollars _[to you know what].

     d.   I will contribute _[something] _[to you know what].

To account grammatically for the kind of variation displayed in (10) one could posit four distinct listemes *contribute*. That approach would fail to capture the generalization of optionality in an explicit fashion. Instead, we will assume that the NI potential associated with any given argument of a predicate is directly captured in the argument structure of the respective lexeme. In other words, a word like *contribute* will be specified with the following argument structure and partially underspecified constraints on argument indices, as informally depicted in (11) and fully developed in Section 3.2.

---

[3] In FrameNet annotation practice, verbs like *sweat, piss, pee, belch, burb, bleed*, etc. would be considered to represent obligatory NI of the Excreta frame element. We do not pursue the possibility of truly obligatory null complementation, which in any case would require no analysis beyond that needed for the semantic interpretation of the obligatory NI argument, as in e.g. Section 3.6.

[4] We are for the moment ignoring implicit arguments that are not NI, i.e. *pro* arguments; see Section 2.3.

(11)　Argument structure for *contribute*

　　　⟨ $NP_{x:\neg NI}$, $NP_{y:\neg DNI}$, $PP_{z:\neg INI}$ ⟩

The intuition is that *contribute* selects a list of three arguments, the first of which, in a finite clause, is an NP that cannot be NI (i.e. its referent must be introduced by an overt subject phrase). The verb *contribute* in addition subcategorizes for an NP direct object that cannot be DNI (i.e. it must either be referential or INI), and an oblique that cannot be INI (i.e. it must either be referential or DNI). Thus, if the latter two arguments are not overtly realized, they are required to be interpreted existentially or anaphorically, respectively. However, there are a variety of contexts that interact with a lexeme's argument structure and license otherwise illicit NI patterns.

2.2　Contextually Licensed NI

There are cases in which features of the discourse context, including narrative context and shared background knowledge, allow a predicator to exhibit NI potential it does not possess inherently. The verb *pull* does not, in general, license DNI, as illustrated in the following excerpt from a hearing of a commission of the US Congress.

(12)　[@]Mr. Blanton: Had your little girl pulled this fire-alarm box that you know of?

　　　Mr. Puliam: No, sir; and nobody had seen her pull *(it).

　　　Mr. Blanton: And they just suspected she had pulled *(it)?

　　　Mr. Puliam: The fire-alarm box had been pulled and my children were seen around there.

　　　Mr. Blanton: And the child could have pulled *(it)?

　　　Mr. Puliam: Yes, sir.

　　　Mr. Blanton: And there are some 66,000 other children in the District who could have pulled *(it)?

However, in a situation of sufficient immediacy and salience, the object of a verb like *pull* or *push*, which does not inherently license DNI, may remain implicit. (13) and (14) illustrate (object and subject) DNI of this kind, which we dub *Accessibility DNI*.

(13)　a.　I leaped to my feet and stumbled toward her. My fingers grabbed for the deadly necklace. I pulled ∅ with all my strength. Snap! (Stine, undated)

　　　b.　Ernesto pointed again to the rocks. "Learn not to push ∅ before the right moment," he said. (Stein, 1958)

   c.   Suddenly the boulder was rocking and Tola Beg pushed Ø hard, pushed Ø with all the strength he had in his old body and with all the strength he had in his mind. (L'Amour, 2001, 36)

(14) a.   So, how's Julia?
      Ø Broke her arm, and hit her head pretty badly. She's in the hospital for observation. (Crichton, 2002, 157)

     b. [@](Your guy gets to the plate, kicks in the sand, knocks his shoes with the bat. He always does that.) Ø Takes his stance. Ø Gets comfortable. Ø Looks at the pitcher for the first time.

     c. [@]Announcer: And he's behind Lehtonen, 3 seconds left, Ø passes it to Sutton, and THE THRASHERS WIN 2–0.

We take the key concept at work in licensing this kind of NI to be the *accessibility* of an intended referent (Ariel, 2001; Gregory & Michaelis, 2001). Accessibility is conceived as a gradient property: the degree to which "the speaker can predict or could have predicted that a particular linguistic item will or would occur in a particular position within a sentence" (Prince, 1981a, 226).

Ruppenhofer & Michaelis (2010) note that generic, including habitual, aspect can also license INI of the direct object of a simple transitive verb, while this is not possible under other circumstances. Consider for example the contrast in (15). Ruppenhofer and Michaelis refer to such cases as *dispositional INI*.

(15) a. * The cops arrested Ø last night.
      (Ruppenhofer & Michaelis, 2014, 159)

     b. Sure, the cops arrest Ø when they can, but it's always in small amounts.
      (Ruppenhofer & Michaelis, 2014, 159)

As we discuss in what follows, we adopt the dispositional operator proposed by Boneh (2019), which yields habitual, generic, or disposition readings depending on circumstances. Disposition attributions are statements that ascribe to an entity an inherent property that may remain unrealized unless the right conditions obtain. Dispositional DNI is not limited to direct objects, as the attested datum in (16) shows.

(16) [@]He or she is a philanthropist and gives Ø Ø whenever asked for assistance.

Another contextual licensor of NI is the *instructional imperative*, which allows the DNI suppression of an object in imperative constructions expressing instructions. This is illustrated in (17). In this genre, the context must be such that the theme under discussion is the topic of the utterance, which assures the possibility of a DNI interpretation.

(17) a. Method: Blend all the ingredients in an electric blender. Serve $\emptyset$ cold.
          (Ruppenhofer & Michaelis, 2010, 106)

      b. Chill $\emptyset_i$ before serving $\emptyset_i$.
          (Ruppenhofer & Michaelis, 2010, 159)

      c. In a bowl, toss $\emptyset_i$ with salt and set $\emptyset_i$ aside.
          (Ruppenhofer & Michaelis, 2014, 72)

      d. In a skillet, sauté $\emptyset_i$ until browned $\emptyset_i$ but not crisp $\emptyset_i$.
          (Ruppenhofer & Michaelis, 2014, 72)

Ruppenhofer & Michaelis (2010) observe that NI is licensed by several other genres, such as "labelese," diary style, sports reporting ("match reports"), and certain nonquotative verbs used quotatively. For all of these, NI is of the deictic/anaphoric – that is, DNI, variety and in some cases targets erstwhile subjects. Example (18a) illustrates labelese and (18b, c) illustrate the diary genre.[5]

(18) a. $\emptyset$ Contains alcohol.
          (Ruppenhofer & Michaelis, 2010, 160)

      b. $\emptyset$ Woke up, $\emptyset$ fought with Marge... $\emptyset$ ate Guatemalan insanity peppers...
          [COCA, TV 1997]

One final instance of contextual NI that we will consider is observed in the omission of the oblique argument in short passives, illustrated in the minimal pair in (19). The agent of *fed* is unexpressed in (19b). We will argue that whether

---

[5] Although genre-restricted subject ellipsis in languages that, like English, do not allow anaphoric subject ellipsis as a general matter, it has been well studied in relation to diary corpora (e.g. Haegeman & Ihsane [2001]), the phenomenon is not exclusively restricted to diary contexts, as also noted by Haegeman & Ihsane (2001), who cite several, presumably invented but highly plausible, examples from the earlier literature. Example (i) is due to Richard Oehrle (p.c., cited in Kay [2002]). Since the example is also imagined, rather than attested, no context is available, but it seems to present a prima facie candidate for licensing by Accessibility DNI.

(i) [Baseball context] $\emptyset$ Got 'im, $\emptyset$ struck 'im out!

the oblique argument is overtly realized depends on the cognitive status of the demoted agent.

(19) a. The iguanas were properly fed by Robin.

      b. The iguanas were properly fed $\emptyset$.

2.3 Constructionally Bound Implicit Arguments

Whereas NI involves implicit arguments whose semantic value is determined directly from context independently of anything else in the logical structure of the sentence, there are also cases where implicit arguments derive part of their semantic value from elsewhere in the linguistic representation, and therefore are more syntactically active. Such implicit arguments resemble NI but differ from it in that their interpretation is constrained by some aspect of the grammar, rather than by discourse context. This is the case of controlled *pro* examples like (20a,b), which are co-referential with a structurally higher argument, and other constructions such as implicit subjects of dangling participles like (20c), as well as imperative subjects like (20d).

(20) a. I [made [the top]$_x$ [$\emptyset_x$ go into the cup]].

      b. I$_x$ love [$\emptyset_x$ to play this game].

      c. $\emptyset_x$ Sitting on a park bench, Sam$_x$ watched the kids play.

      d. $\emptyset$ Get me another cup please.

Each of the constructions responsible for governing the reference of these *pro* arguments imposes a different constraint. For example, in (20c) the implicit subject is required to be the subject of the matrix, whereas in (20d) the subject is assigned the same semantic content as the pronoun *you*, and is omitted.

   Remarkably, such implicit *pro* arguments can be displaced by a construction. For instance, in (21a) the object of *please* is extracted and linked to the implicit inverted subject of the imperative. Analogously, in (21b) the *pro* object is extracted to the subject position in the ARG-ST. In (21c) the implicit object of *fed* is passivized, promoted to the subject argument of the dangling participle, and in (21d) the implicit object is extracted from the object phrase and corresponds to the object of the preposition *of*. Finally, in (21e) a *pro* theme of *won* can be extracted, and co-indexed with the nominal head *prize*.

(21) a. Don't $\emptyset_x$ be so hard to please $\_x$.
          (Huddleston & Pullum, 2002, 1086)

      b. $\emptyset_x$ Being especially easy to talk to $\_x$, Pat$_x$ was able to escape being laid off.

   c.   If $\emptyset_x$ properly fed, Iguanas$_x$ can live for a long time.

   d.   If $\emptyset_x$ taken good care of $\_\_x$, Iguanas$_x$ can live for a long time.

   e.   The prize$_x$ which$_x$/$\emptyset_x$ I thought you won $\_\_x$ was this one.

Such data suggest that implicit *pro* arguments can still participate in standard alternations, like their overt counterparts. This contrasts with NI, which disallows displacement as illustrated in (22). Thus, (22a) cannot be interpreted as a content question (only as a polar question), and (22b) is illicit.

(22)   a. *$\emptyset_x$ Did Robin win $\_\_x$?

          ($\neq$ 'What$_x$ did Robin win $\_\_x$?')

     b. *$\emptyset_x$ Is easy to talk to $\_\_x$.

          (cf. 'Sam$_x$ is easy to talk to $\_\_x$.)

We also assume that arbitrary *pro* constructions like those in (23) also involve a *pro* argument rather than an NI argument, given that such implicit arbitrary referents have a generic import. We assume this import comes from being bound to a covert generic quantifier that is introduced via a lexical rule.[6]

(23)   a. $\emptyset$ To err is human.

     b. It is forbidden $\emptyset$ to smoke.

     c. The Titanic was easier $\emptyset$ to sink than anyone imagined.

Bhatt and Pancheva (2006) point out that the fact that some implicit arguments have syntactic effects, while others don't, is theoretically disturbing, and the line between the two classes is not agreed upon. In our view, the relation between NI arguments and *pro* arguments is the one summed up in (24).

(24) **The NI/*pro* Generalization:**

- NI arguments are not bound in the logical structure of the sentence.
- Pro arguments are bound in the logical structure of the sentence.

---

[6] Other constructions that likely involve an arbitrary *pro* are those involving dangling gerunds, like (i) and (ii). At first glance, these suggest the implicit subject is the speaker, but the continuation in example (ii) suggests that this tendency is merely an inferential one, and not strictly grammatically enforced.

   i. $\emptyset$ Considering the book's popularity, there will likely be a movie adaptation.

  ii. $\emptyset$ Judging by the reviews, that restaurant has slow service, but my experience is very different.

Landau (2010) makes a distinction between Strong Implicit Argument (SIA) and Weak Implicit Argument (WIA), but the empirical basis for such a categorization is problematic (Michelioudakis, 2021). Consider the supposed contrast in (25). Landau's claim is that the passive agent of *played* is a WIA because it is not present in syntactic structure, and therefore *shoeless* cannot be predicated of it.

(25) a.   The game was played [PRO wearing no shoes].

      b. *The game was played shoeless.
         (Landau, 2010, 360)

We note that a verbatim Google search on 9/5/21 for *was played shoeless* produced many examples like "The game was played shoeless," "Previous shot was played shoeless and sockless from a water hazard," and "But the entire regional qualification process in Mexico was played shoeless." Even more frequent is the string *was played barefoot*, yielding examples like (26).[7]

(26) @Players will take the soccer fields with no shoes. The inaugural event held in 2017 was played barefoot, with the money going to children without shoes through Soles 4 Souls.

Landau (2010) relies on well-known contrasts such as (27) to argue for a distinction between WIA and SIA. But the verb *eat* is arguably ambiguous between an intransitive verb denoting a social event, and a transitive verb denoting a manner of consumption. See Glass (2021) for corpus evidence suggesting that such verbs omit their objects more often in the communities where they are more strongly associated with a routine. If so, then the oddness of (26b) follows from attaching an adjective to an intransitive verb.

(27) a.   John ate (the meat).

      b.   John ate *(the meat) raw.

This view is also consistent with the fact that the transitive use of *eat* seems to allow object NI in certain constructions:

(28) These are just a few of the people who are eating Ø raw. ... Each person has different reasons for eating raw.
     [COCA 2005 MAG TotalHealth]

---

[7] See Müller (2008) for evidence that words like *barefoot* are adjectives, contra Chomsky (1986, 211).

3 Formalization

As discussed in the previous section, NI is licensed by certain lexical items but not by others that are semantically very similar, and there are specific genres and constructions that license NI of arguments that otherwise cannot be NI. In the theory we pursue in this section, all of these NI patterns result from the same underlying mechanism, as it interacts with lexical entries and particular lexical constructions, accounting for a range of patterns and predictions that to our knowledge have not previously been explicitly accounted for in the literature. In Section 3.1 we provide a brief introduction to Sign-Based Construction Grammar (SBCG), which is well suited for the phenomena at hand. For more detailed introductions to SBCG see Michaelis (2012) and Sag (2012). With this preparation, we offer a detailed English grammar fragment of lexically licensed null instantiation phenomena in Section 3.2, an account of contextually licensed NI in Section 3.3, and of how displacement phenomena interact with implicit arguments in Section 3.5. Finally, in Section 3.6, we turn to the semantic interpretation of NI arguments.

3.1 Sign-Based Construction Grammar

Sign-Based Construction Grammar takes all linguistic objects like words and phrases to be bundles of phonological, morphosyntactic, semantic, and pragmatic information – that is, Sausurean *signs*. Like its predecessors, SBCG seeks to explicitly characterize the infinite set of signs that constitutes a language in a declarative, constraint-based fashion. Signs are modeled as typed feature structures, represented as Attribute Value Matrices (AVMs) like the one in (29).

$$(29) \quad \begin{bmatrix} sign \\ \text{PHON} & phonological\text{-}object \\ \text{FORM} & morphological\text{-}object \\ \text{SYN} & syntactic\text{-}object \\ \text{SEM} & linguistic\text{-}meaning \\ \text{CNTXT} & context\text{-}object \end{bmatrix}$$

An AVM is a set of attribute–value pairs, representing a function from a set of attributes to a set of types of feature structure. For example, the AVM in (29) denotes a set of feature structures typed as *sign*, and as such it comes with a set of attribute–value pairs each of which specifies a different kind of information. A sign therefore contains information about sound (PHON), morphological form (FORM), syntax (SYN), meaning (SEM), and context (CNTXT). Attributes are written in small caps and types are written in lowercase italics. Unlike the complex feature structures such as (29), represented by AVMs, other feature structure types are atomic. Examples are *accusative, finite*, "–," and "+."

Signs are arranged in a multiple-inheritance hierarchy, as illustrated in (30), whereby all the subtypes of *sign* inherit the attribute–value pairs that are appropriate for signs, as shown in (29), as well as additional constraints distinguishing the subtypes.

(30)

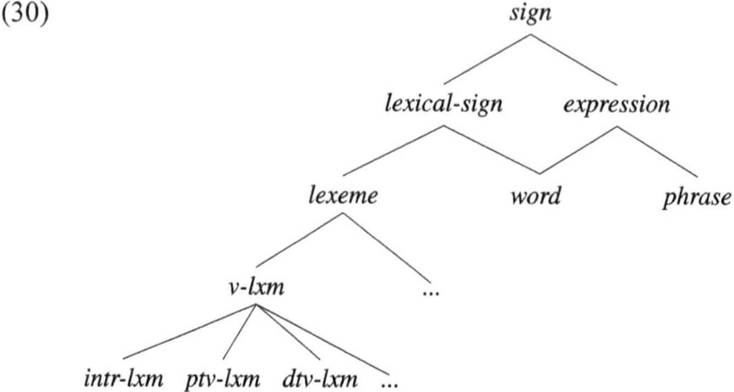

For example, only signs of type *expression*, whose subtypes include the types *word* and *phrase*, but not *lexeme*, are allowed in syntactic constructions (preventing lexemes from appearing in syntax), and only signs of the type *lexical-sign* are allowed in lexical rules. More specifically, morphological derivation rules map signs of type *lexeme* to signs of type *lexeme*, and inflectional rules map signs of type *lexeme* to signs of type *word*. The fact that the type *word* inherits the properties of both *lexical-sign* and *expression* illustrates the *multiple* inheritance property. The type *lexeme* is the supertype of a rich ontology of lexemes, organized in terms of cross-cutting classes (*intr-lxm* for intransitive lexemes, *ptv-lxm* for prepositional transitive, *dtv-lxm* for ditransitive lexemes, etc.), called the hierarchical lexicon (Flickinger, 1987). Analogous subhierarchies exist for nonverbal lexeme classes, which are not shown here due to space limitations. See Sag (2012) for a more detailed discussion. For example, in (31), we show the lexeme for *contribute*, a subtype of *pvt-lxm*, as it is listed in the lexicon.

(31)
$$
\begin{bmatrix}
\textit{contribute-lxm} \\
\text{FORM } \langle \textit{contribute} \rangle \\
\text{SEM} \begin{bmatrix} \text{INDEX} & S \\ \text{FRAMES} & \left\langle \begin{bmatrix} \textit{contribute-fr} \\ \text{SIT } & S \end{bmatrix} \right\rangle \end{bmatrix}
\end{bmatrix}
$$

As in HPSG, signs of type *lexical-sign* introduce one additional feature to what we see in (31), called ARG-ST, which takes lists of signs as its value, and encodes the number, type, and order of arguments that a given sign subcategorizes, regardless of whether such arguments are realized in situ or ex situ, or remain covert, including those interpreted via NI. The members of ARG-ST appear in order of increasing obliqueness, reflecting Keenan and Comrie's Accessibility Hierarchy (Keenan & Comrie, 1977). Sag, Wasow, and Bender (2003, 241) and Ginzburg and Sag (2000, 20-22), general constraints over classes and subclasses of lexemes are responsible for instantiating ARG-ST values in lexemes. In (32), we provide the constraints that are relevant for prepositional transitive verbal lexemes like *contribute* in (31), which we assume are also responsible for binding the indices in FRAMES to the appropriate arguments. Generally, constraints like (32) are of the form $\tau \Rightarrow \phi$ (where τ is some type and ϕ is an AVM feature structure description) and impose restrictions on lexical classes, syntactic structure, semantic composition, phonological structure, morphology, and so on. Here we assume that the lexeme type *contribute-lxm* (among others) is a subtype of *prepositional-transitive-verb-[to]-lexeme* (abbreviated as *ptv[to]-lxm*), which in turn is a subtype of a larger family of lexeme types, *ptv-lxm*. Each of these types imposes constraints that vary in granularity, and subtypes inherit all the constraints of their supertypes.

(32)   a.

$$ptv\text{-}lxm \Rightarrow \begin{bmatrix} \text{ARG-ST} \left\langle \text{NP}[\text{INDEX } X], \text{NP}[\text{INDEX } Y], \text{PP}[\text{INDEX } Z] \right\rangle \\ \text{SEM} \begin{bmatrix} \text{FRAMES} \left\langle \begin{bmatrix} \text{FES } \langle X, Y, Z \rangle \end{bmatrix}, ... \right\rangle \end{bmatrix} \end{bmatrix}$$

     b.

$$ptv[to]\text{-}lxm \Rightarrow \begin{bmatrix} \text{ARG-ST} \left\langle ..., \begin{bmatrix} \text{MARKING} & to \end{bmatrix} \right\rangle \end{bmatrix}$$

In words, (32a) states that every sign of the type *ptv-lxm* bears the subcategorization frame $\langle \text{NP}_x, \text{NP}_y, \text{PP}_z \rangle$.[8] Note that F(RAME-)E(LEMENT)S values are lists of indices,[9] while ARG-ST values are lists of signs. The constraint in (32a) thus specifies the value of ARG-ST and F(RAME-)E(LEMENT)S of all verbal lexemes that

---

[8]   Here we adopt a slightly different encoding for semantic arguments than that of standard SBCG, as a matter of convenience later in the Element, but nothing truly hinges on this choice. In a nutshell, the feature F(RAME) E(LEMENT)S – a term borrowed from FrameNet (Fillmore, Johnson, & Petruck, 2003) – lists the semantic indices that a given predicator takes. An analogous feature named SEMANTIC-ARGUMENTS was proposed by Koenig (1999), in Head-Driven Phrase Structure Grammar. See (34) for an illustration of how FES relate to a more standard, first-order logic notation.

[9]   Readers familiar with the frame-semantic tradition may be bothered by the absence of names for the frame elements. We assume each frame specifies which semantic role constraints attach to each of its indices (i.e. each frame element introduces the features INDEX and ROLE and, since semantic role names need not be referred to elsewhere in the formal representation, they need not be made part of it.

correspond to prepositional transitive verbs, or more technically, resolves the underspecified values of ARG-ST and FES for all lexemes typed as instances of *ptv-lxm*. The constraint in (32b) states that the *ptv[to]-lxm* subtype of *ptv-lxm* further requires that the most oblique argument be marked with the preposition *to*. Other sister types of *ptv[to]-lxm* impose different marking patterns, all of which share the constraints imposed by *ptv-lxm*. In the case of the *contribute-lxm* sign in (31), this results in the lexeme shown in (33). The result is a lexeme that selects a subject NP, a direct object, and an oblique object, as seen in (33).

$$(33) \quad \begin{bmatrix} \textit{contribute-lxm} \\ \text{FORM} \ \langle \textit{contribute} \rangle \\ \text{SEM} \begin{bmatrix} \text{INDEX} \quad S \\ \text{FRAMES} \quad \left\langle \begin{bmatrix} \textit{contribute-fr} \\ \text{SIT} \ S \\ \text{FES} \ \langle X, Y, Z \rangle \end{bmatrix} \right\rangle \end{bmatrix} \\ \text{ARG-ST} \ \left\langle \text{NP[INDEX } Z], \text{ NP[INDEX } Y], \text{ PP} \begin{bmatrix} \text{MARKING} \quad to \\ \text{INDEX} \quad Z \end{bmatrix} \right\rangle \end{bmatrix}$$

Semantically, the verb denotes a predication of the form $contribute\,(s,x,y,z)$, if rendered in a more standard first-order logic notation, which we encode in terms of a frame. In general, we have the correspondence in (34), for any given frame predicate name P with n arguments (i.e. frame elements).

$$(34) \quad P(s,x_1,...,x_n) \quad \text{is encoded as} \quad \begin{bmatrix} \textit{P-fr} \\ \text{SIT} \quad S \\ \text{FES} \quad \langle X_1,...,X_n \rangle \end{bmatrix}$$

In (32a), the order of elements in the ARG-ST value is the same as the order of the elements in the FES value of the first frame. This co-alignment is dictated by the fact that we do not distinguish individual frame elements by naming them. The fact that we order the frame elements to match the order of syntactic obliqueness may give the impression of a tacit assumption that the syntactic properties of an argument determine its semantic properties. Nothing of the sort is intended. The ordering of the FES value to match that of the ARG-ST value is simply a matter of notational necessity. On the contrary, we are aware of the long tradition of serious efforts to derive the principle syntactic properties of a predicate's arguments from its semantics – that is, linking theory (Bresnan & Zaenen, 1990; Goldberg, 2019; Grimshaw, 1990; Levin, 1993;

Levin, 1985). For a theory of argument linking particularly appropriate to the present approach see Davis (2001), Koenig and Davis (2003, 2006), and Davis, Koenig, and Wechsler (2021).

There are various other lexemic constraints at work, such as the one in (35). In the case of English, the first member of a verbal ARG-ST list is the EXTERNAL ARGUMENT (XARG), which has a number of special properties, as described in what follows. Thus, (35) applies to all verbal lexemes to state their part-of-speech and to single out the first member of the ARG-ST list as being the external argument.

(35)
$$v\text{-}lxm \Rightarrow \begin{bmatrix} \text{SYN} & \begin{bmatrix} \text{CAT} & \begin{bmatrix} verb \\ \text{XARG} & K \\ \text{LID} & L \end{bmatrix} \end{bmatrix} \\ \text{SEM} & \begin{bmatrix} \text{FRAMES } L \end{bmatrix} \\ \text{ARG-ST} & \langle K, ... \rangle \end{bmatrix}$$

Italicized capitals are variables over feature structures, and so the presence of two such occurrences in (35) means that the value of XARG is the same sign as the first member of ARG-ST. The members of a FRAMES list always form a single-rooted tree with respect to the binary relation according to which one frame serves, via its LABEL value, as an argument of another frame. The initial frame of a list is the root of the tree. The value of the feature L(EXICAL)ID(ENTITY), on the other hand, is the entire list of frames of a lexeme. In a headed phrase the LID is visible at every level of "projection," and thus allows for the selection of a complement to be constrained by the identity of the lexical head, as in *rely on/*in her, trust *on/in her*.

The sign singled out by XARG has a number of special properties in English. This is the only argument that can bear nominative case, is suppressed in passive although optionally available as an oblique complement headed by the preposition *by*, appears immediately postverbally in inverted clauses, serves as the target of control and raising, binds the pronominal subject of a sentence tag (36a), participates in the binding relation between an dangling participle subject and an element of the main clause (36b,c), etcetera. The last two properties illustrate the fact that the XARG is the only argument that can participate in a dependency with an item outside its clause.[10]

---

[10] The possible values of XARG are *sign* and *none*. The XARG of an NP, if there is one, is the genitive determiner, which is enforced by a further lexemic constraint; see Sag (2012) for more details.

(36) a. The guests$_x$ left, didn't they$_x$?

b. $\emptyset_x$ Having caught sight of each other$_x$, the kids$_x$ started laughing.

c. Which kid$_x$ did you say that – with his$_x$ parents out of town – $\_x$ would not be too hard to convince $\_x$ to host a party?

The ARG-ST feature is restricted to *lexical signs* – that is, *lexemes* and *words* – but the XARG, as a CATegory feature (analogous to the HEAD feature of HPSG) is visible at all levels of a headed *phrase*. For completeness, the effect of applying (35) to (33) is shown in (37). In reality, all constraints apply simultaneously, and therefore (37) is the result of simultaneously combining (31), (32), and (35). The notation $K{:}\phi$ means that the value of the variable K has at least the information described by ϕ. Thus, the value of XARG is the same sign that appears at the beginning of the ARG-ST list, and is required to be an NP bearing index X.

(37)

$$
\begin{bmatrix}
\textit{contribute-lxm} \\
\text{FORM } \langle \textit{contribute} \rangle \\[6pt]
\text{SYN } \begin{bmatrix} \text{CAT } \begin{bmatrix} \textit{verb} \\ \text{XARG} & K \\ \text{LID} & L \end{bmatrix} \end{bmatrix} \\[12pt]
\text{SEM } \begin{bmatrix} \text{INDEX} & S \\[6pt] \text{FRAMES} & L : \left\langle \begin{bmatrix} \textit{contribute-fr} \\ \text{SIT} & s \\ \text{FES } \langle X, Y, Z \rangle \end{bmatrix} \right\rangle \end{bmatrix} \\[12pt]
\text{ARG-ST } \left\langle K{:}\text{NP}[\text{INDEX } X],\ \text{NP}[\text{INDEX } Y],\ \text{PP}\begin{bmatrix} \text{MARKING} & \textit{to} \\ \text{INDEX} & Z \end{bmatrix} \right\rangle
\end{bmatrix}
$$

Although the ARG-ST contains the argument structure information of a lexical expression, it says nothing about how each particular argument is to be realized. Those elements of ARG-ST that appear in the feature VAL(ENCE) are to be locally realized, and those that appear in GAP are to be realized ex situ (e.g., clefts, topicalization, wh-interrogatives, etc.). The mapping between ARG-ST and these SYN features is achieved by the Argument Realization Principle (ARP) as shown provisionally in (38), adapted from Ginzburg and Sag (2000, 214) to SBCG. Here, VAL and GAP are lists of signs, like ARG-ST.

(38) **Argument Realization Principle Construction** ($\uparrow$*lexical-sign*) [provisional]

$$
\textit{word} \Rightarrow \begin{bmatrix} \text{SYN} & \begin{bmatrix} \text{VAL} & L_1 \\ \text{GAP} & L_2 \end{bmatrix} \\[6pt] \text{ARG-ST} & L_1 \bigcirc L_2 \end{bmatrix}
$$

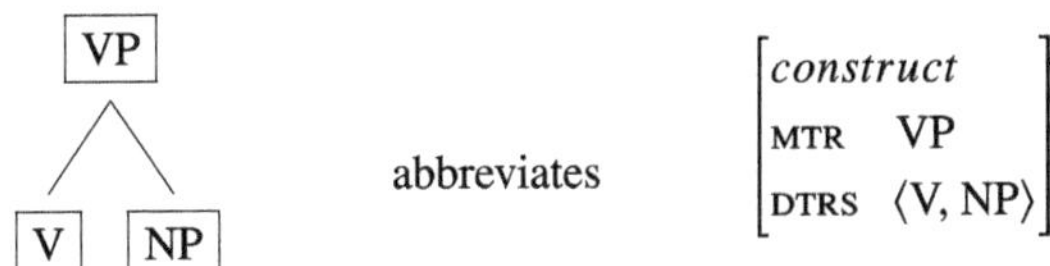

Figure 1 Phrasal constructs encoded as feature structures.

In (38) the ARG-ST list is nondeterministically split into two sublists using the sequence union relation '○' (Kathol, 2001; Reape, 1996), each of which may or may not be empty.[11] In verb–complement constructs, the first member of the mother's VAL is the XARG and the remaining members of the head daughter's VAL are discharged from VAL as complement sisters. In subject–VP constructs, the singleton member of the head daughter's VAL is the XARG and is discharged as a subject phrase. We will have to reformulate (38) in order to accommodate NI, however.

All information is uniformly represented in terms of typed feature structures, including phrasal structure. Thus, the tree on the left-hand side of Figure 1 is represented in terms of the feature structure on the right. The feature MTR singles out the mother node and the list-valued feature DTRS enumerates the immediate daughters of the construction. Constructs, but not signs, have the MTR and DTRS feature.

We will use the notation on the left when depicting structures licensed by the grammar. It is important to note, however, that the symbols "NP" and "VP" are merely abbreviations of feature structure descriptions. Thus, "NP" abbreviates any nominal sign (lexical or phrasal) with saturated (i.e. empty) valence, the reference of which has been determined by a binding quantifier (overtly or covertly).[12] Similarly, "VP" abbreviates any verbal sign (lexical or phrasal) that still has not satisfied the requirement of combining with the external argument. This is shown in (39). Accordingly, "S" abbreviates a verbal sign with saturated valence, and so on.

---

[11] The sequence union relation "○" can combine lists nondeterministically, as if they were sets. Thus $L_1 \bigcirc L_2 = \langle \text{NP,PP} \rangle$ can be resolved in exactly four ways: (i) $L_1 = \langle \rangle$ $L_2 = \langle \text{NP,PP} \rangle$, (ii) $L_1 = \langle \text{NP} \rangle$ $L_2 = \langle \text{PP} \rangle$, (iii) $L_1 = \langle \text{PP} \rangle$ $L_2 = \langle \text{NP} \rangle$, and (iv) $L_1 = \langle \text{NP,PP} \rangle$ $L_2 = \langle \rangle$. See Reape (1996) for details.

[12] Determiners select unmarked nominal heads and bind their discourse referent, yielding in the process a marked nominal phrase (Sag, 2012). We assume that bare nominals are licensed by unary-branching constructions, which add a quantifier to the semantics of the nominal head, yielding an (implicitly) marked nominal sign, and add [MRKG *det(ermined)*] to the mother. For more on unary-branching nominal constructions of various kinds, see Michaelis (2003) and Fillmore (2013).

(39) a.

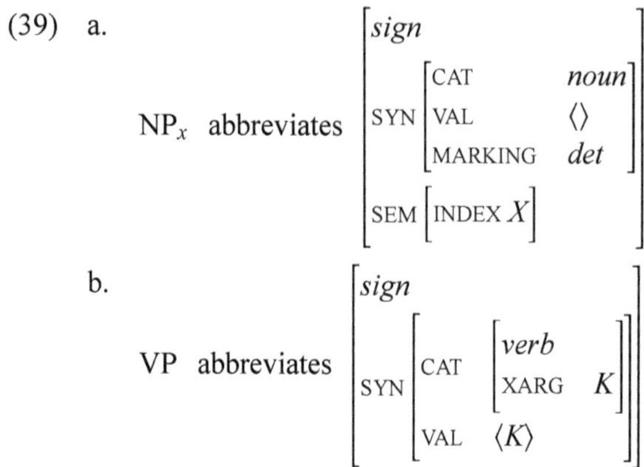

Constructs are defined as introducing exactly two features, MTR and DTRS, as shown in (40), from Sag (2012, 145). Furthermore, the value of the MTR feature is required to be of type *sign*, and the value of DTRS is required to be a non-empty list of signs (i.e. a feature structure of type *n(on)-e(mpty)-list*). In Section 3.2, we revise this constraint so that only overt signs are allowed in MTR and DTRS.[13]

(40) **Type declaration for** *construct* [provisional]

$$construct : \begin{bmatrix} \text{MTR} & sign \\ \text{DTRS} & ne\text{-}list(sign) \end{bmatrix}$$

As in the case of lexeme types, there is a hierarchy of constructional types imposing constraints on the kinds of sign that that form constructs. In lexical constructions, the signs in DTRS are of type *lexical-sign* – that is, either *lexeme* or *word* – and in phrasal constructions they are of type *expression* – that is, either *word* or *phrase*.

The construction (41) from Sag (2012, 152) is responsible for allowing heads to combine with complements (the Predicational Head-Complement Construction; PHCC). The notation $X!\phi$, where ϕ is an AVM, means that ϕ contains

---

[13] Like HPSG, SBSG distinguishes a signature, which sets out the basic types (classes of feature structures) of a grammar, as distinct from the constraints (constructions) that operate on those types. Type declarations are expressed with a colon between the name of a type and an AVM stating which features are appropriate for such type. Constructions are conditional constraints indicated by "⇒," preceded by a type name and followed by an AVM expressing a feature structure description that constrains the aforementioned type (Sag, 2012, 103, 104 note). As Sag remarks, the decision whether to cast a particular generalization as a type declaration of the signature or as a construction is sometimes a matter of choice. In some cases, e.g. (32) and (35), giving the construction a name does not seem necessary. Other terminological choices might, of course, be made to bring the technical use of "construction" in closer relation to its intuitive use, but this Element is probably not an appropriate place for that.

exactly the same information as any AVM τ tagged as $X{:}\tau$ except information that is noted explicitly.[14] Because this is a headed construction (as indicated by the notation ↑*headed-cxt*), there is an additional feature HD-DTR that singles out which member of DTRS is the head sign. The operation "⊕" is the list concatenation relation, which is used to append lists.[15]

(41) **Predicational Head-Complement Construction** (↑*headed-cxt*) [provisional]

$$pred\text{-}hd\text{-}comp\text{-}cxt \Rightarrow \begin{bmatrix} \text{MTR} & \left[\text{SYN } X\,!\left[\text{VAL } \langle Y\rangle\right]\right] \\[2ex] \text{DTRS} & \langle Z\rangle \oplus L{:}ne\text{-}list \\[2ex] \text{HD-DTR } Z: & \begin{bmatrix} word \\[1ex] \text{SYN } X: \begin{bmatrix} \text{CAT} \left[\text{XARG } Y\right] \\[1ex] \text{VAL } \langle Y\rangle \oplus L \end{bmatrix} \end{bmatrix} \end{bmatrix}$$

The constraint in (41) has the effect of requiring that the first daughter be a lexical head, and that all subsequent local sisters correspond to signs that are lexically subcategorized by the head. Thus, if the first member of DTRS bears a VAL(ENCE) specification like $\langle NP_x, NP_y, PP_z\rangle$ then $Y = NP_x$ (the external argument), and $L = \langle NP_y, PP_z\rangle$, licensing a VP like the one shown in Figure 2. Thus, whereas the head daughter is [VAL $\langle NP_x, NP_y, PP_z\rangle$], the mother is specified as [VAL $\langle NP_x\rangle$].

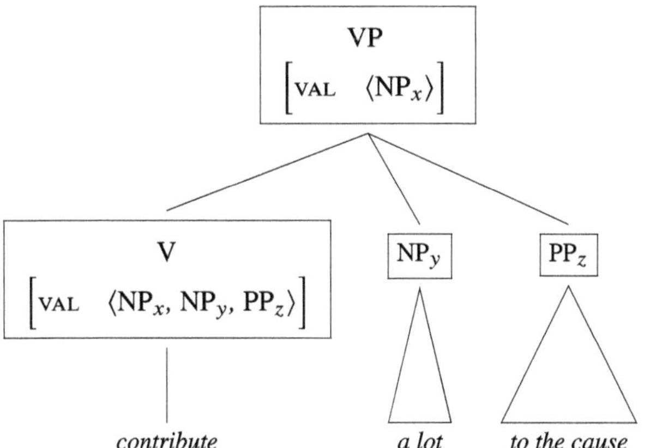

Figure 2 The VP *contribute a lot to the cause* (abbreviated).

---

[14] See Sag (2012, 125) for fuller discussion of this notation.

[15] In Section 3.5, we adopt a reformulated version of the PHCC.

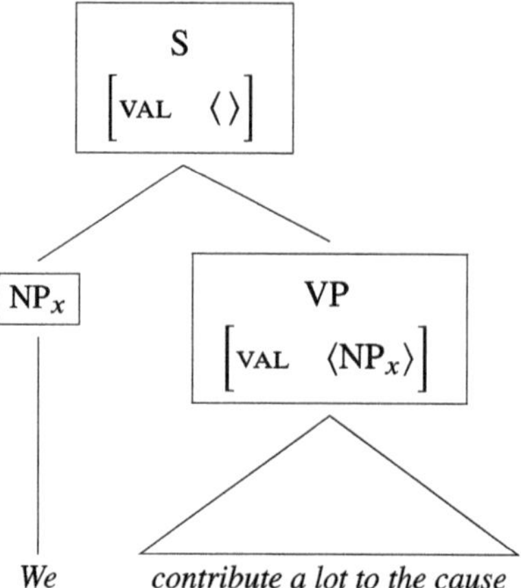

Figure 3 The clause *We contribute a lot to the cause* (abbreviated).

Another example of a headed construction is shown in (42), which is responsible for combining an external argument with a verb phrase. Here, the second daughter is the head, which is required to be a finite, noninverted verb form, compatible with a nonauxiliary construction.[16] The result is a verbal sign that is fully saturated – that is, a clause.

(42)   **Subject-Predicate Construction** (↑*headed-cxt*)

$$\textit{subj-pred-cxt} \Rightarrow \begin{bmatrix} \text{MTR} & \begin{bmatrix} \text{SYN } X! \begin{bmatrix} \text{VAL } \langle\rangle \end{bmatrix} \end{bmatrix} \\ \text{DTRS} & \langle Y, Z \rangle \\ \text{HD-DTR } Z : \begin{bmatrix} \text{SYN } X : \begin{bmatrix} \text{CAT} \begin{bmatrix} \text{VF} & \textit{fin} \\ \text{INV} & - \\ \text{AUX} & - \\ \text{XARG} & Y \end{bmatrix} \\ \text{VAL } \langle Y \rangle \end{bmatrix} \end{bmatrix} \end{bmatrix}$$

The Subject-Predicate Construction licenses structures like the one in Figure 3, where a subject NP is combined with its subcategorizing VP sister, to yield a clause.

Following Ginzburg and Sag (2000, 45), we require the root node of a clause to be verbal, finite, and bear empty VAL and GAP specifications, as specified in (43):

---

[16] As detailed in Sag (2012) and Sag et al. (2020) nonauxiliary verbs are specified as [INV −] (making them noninvertible) and as [AUX −], whereas most auxiliary verbs are underspecified for INV and AUX.

(43)

$$\mathrm{S}_{root} = \left[\mathrm{SYN} \begin{bmatrix} \mathrm{CAT} \begin{bmatrix} verb \\ \mathrm{VF} \quad fin \end{bmatrix} \\ \mathrm{VAL}\ \langle\rangle \\ \mathrm{GAP}\ \langle\rangle \end{bmatrix} \right]$$

Various other constraints come into play in SBCG, some of which are discussed later in this Element, as they have a more direct bearing on our analysis of NI. For our purposes, the present discussion suffices to illustrate the basic mechanics of the formalism and of the theory.

3.2 Lexically Licensed Null Instantiation

As discussed, lexically licensed null instantiation is optional and exhibits lexeme-specific patterns. The verb *contribute* allows the object to undergo INI and the PP to undergo DNI, and therefore have paradigmatic examples like (10), repeated here as (44).

(44)   a.   I will contribute ten dollars to your campaign.

        b.   I will contribute _[something] to your campaign.

        c.   I will contribute ten dollars _[to you know what].

        d.   I will contribute _[something] _[to you know what].

In order to capture these facts explicitly, we assume that the NI potential associated with any given argument of a predicate is directly encoded in the argument structure of the corresponding lexeme. We further assume along with Pollard and Sag (1994) that semantic indices are organized in a multiple-inheritance type hierarchy, forming a taxonomy of semantic indices, which we extend as shown in (45), in order to represent the optionality of NI perspicuously.

(45)

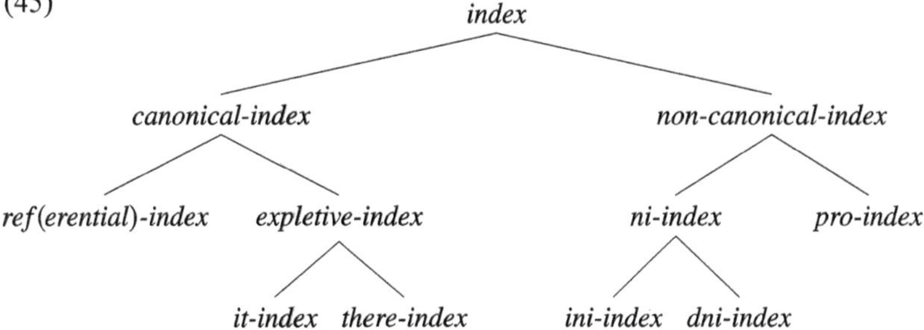

According to this hierarchy, there are two major kinds of index: canonical and noncanonical. Canonical indices correspond to the expletive (semantically vacuous) indices introduced by the dummy pronouns *it* and *there*, as well as the semantically active indices occurring in overtly realized arguments. Noncanonical indices, on the other hand, can be of the NI variety, in which case they are interpreted contextually, without an explicitly overt correlate, or *pro*-indices, which are unexpressed in signs functioning as raised, controlled, or "arbitrarily" interpreted arguments. This organization of indices will play a key role in allowing us to use underspecification to constrain the NI potential of particular arguments.

We model indices via an INDEX feature that includes an AGReement feature (Pollard & Sag, 1994; Wechsler & Zlatic, 2003) and a D(ISCOURSE-)R(EFERENT) feature, as in Kamp and Reyle (1993) and Iordăchioaia and Richter (2015). For example, the INDEX information associated with the pronoun *she* is shown in (46). The types *expletive-index* are specified as [DR *none*], which automatically ensures that no expletive index can appear in the FES list. Since we use capital variables $X...Z$ for INDEX values, lower case letters $x...z$ are reserved for the discourse referent variables.

$$
(46) \quad \left[\text{INDEX} \; \left[\begin{array}{l} \textit{ref-index} \\[4pt] \text{AGR} \; \left[\begin{array}{ll} \text{PER} & \textit{3rd} \\ \text{NUM} & \textit{sing} \\ \text{GEN} & \textit{fem} \end{array} \right] \\[12pt] \text{DR} \quad x \end{array} \right] \right]
$$

We assume that semantic representations with free discourse referent variables are not interpretable, and therefore infelicitous. Hence, for a discourse referent variable to obtain a value it must either be explicitly assigned one via an equality (e.g. $x = robin$) or via a quantifier. The *ni-index* discourse referent variable are special in that they will be assigned values during interpretation, without the presence of a quantifier in the semantic representation (Farkas & de Swart, 2003, ch. 3).[17] The interpretation of signs bearing *ini-index* or *dni-index* is discussed in Section 3.6. Next, we reformulate the sign type hierarchy in (30) slightly, as shown in (47), so that it becomes possible to distinguish between covert signs, which do not have any phonology or morphological form, and overt signs, which do. Thus, overt signs are morphophonologically potent lexemes, words, and phrases.[18]

---

[17] This means that *pro-index* discourse referent variables are interpretable only if they are bound to a referent, either via control (e.g. *Sam [made [Robin]$_x$ [Ø$_x$ sing]]*), via an implicit equality (e.g. *Ø (= addressee) go home!*), or an implicit quantifier (e.g. *It's easy Ø (= for anyone) to say that*).

[18] The sign type hierarchy of Bender (1999) distinguishes between covert and overt signs, but provides no principled account of lexemic NI, nor does it distinguish between DNI and INI.

(47)

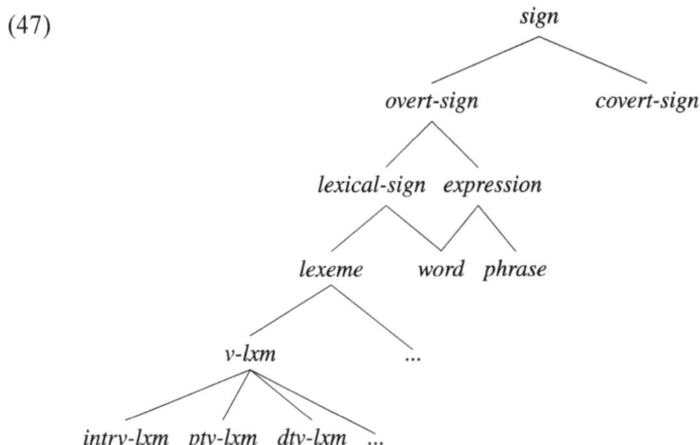

We formalize the differing constraints on overt and covert signs in (48) by stating that the type *sign* introduces morphosyntactic, semantic, and pragmatic features, and that the type *overt-sign* in addition introduces morphophonological features. In other words, any feature structure of type *overt-sign* comes with PHON and FORM information; it also comes with SYN, SEM, and CNTXT information, via inheritance from the type *sign*.

(48)

a.

$$\textit{sign} : \begin{bmatrix} \text{SYN} & \textit{syn-object} \\ \text{SEM} & \textit{linguistic-meaning} \\ \text{CNTXT} & \textit{context-object} \end{bmatrix}$$

b.

$$\textit{overt-sign} : \begin{bmatrix} \text{PHON} & \textit{phon-object} \\ \text{FORM} & \textit{morph-object} \end{bmatrix}$$

Thus, overt signs have the full set of features introduced in Sag (2012, 180), since they carry morphosyntactic information including the FORM and PHONology.[19] Covert signs, on the other hand, do not carry the features FORM and PHONology.

The conditional constraints in (49) specify that overt signs are required to have canonical indices (i.e. an *expletive-index* or a *referential-index*), and covert signs are required to have noncanonical indices (i.e. a *dni-index*, *ini-index* or *pro-index*).

(49)   a.   *overt-sign* $\Rightarrow$ [SEM [INDEX *canonical-index*]]

       b.   *covert-sign* $\Rightarrow$ [SEM [INDEX *noncanonical-index*]]

---

[19] Since phonology is never at issue in this Element, we omit PHON in all subsequent AVMs.

Something must require the daughters of syntactic phrasal constructions in SBCG to be typed as *overt-sign*, preventing covert signs of any kind from appearing in syntax as silent phrasal nodes. To this end, we reformulate in (50) Sag's (2012, 106) type constraint over constructs shown in (40). This type declaration ensures that all overt phrases in English are canonical – that is, either *referential, it*, or *there*.

(50)   **Type declaration for** *construct*

$$construct : \begin{bmatrix} \text{MTR} & \textit{overt-sign} \\ \text{DTRS} & \textit{ne-list}(\textit{overt-sign}) \end{bmatrix}$$

Finally, recall that the ARP in (38) is the constraint responsible for mapping ARG-ST specifications to VAL and GAP. Whereas the VAL feature lists in situ arguments of a predicate (e.g. subjects and objects in their usual locations), the GAP feature lists the ex situ arguments (e.g. topicalized, relativized, and interrogative arguments). We reformulate the constraint in (38) as shown in (51). The ARG-ST list is nondeterministically split into three sublists using the sequence union relation "◯" (Kathol, 2001; Reape, 1996), each of which may or may not be empty. One sublist of arguments corresponds to VAL (i.e. locally realized arguments), another sublist corresponds to GAP (i.e. extracted arguments), and a third sublist that must consist exclusively of *covert* signs (signs that will not be overt).

(51)   **Argument Realization Principle Construction** ($\uparrow$*lexical-sign*) [revised]

$$word \Rightarrow \begin{bmatrix} \text{ARG-ST} & L_1 \bigcirc L_2 \bigcirc \textit{list}\left(\textit{covert-sign}\right) \\ \\ \text{SYN} & \begin{bmatrix} \text{VAL} & L_1 \\ \text{GAP} & L_2 \end{bmatrix} \end{bmatrix}$$

Although *pro-index* and *ni-index* signs can appear in VAL(ENCE) and GAP, they cannot be discharged from those lists as per the definition of construct in (50), as only *overt* signs can appear in DTRS. Allowing *pro-index* signs in VAL allows us to license cases where an implicit argument is controlled by a predicator, and allowing such signs in GAP allows us to displace such arguments.[20] More specifically, the occurrence of a sign typed *covert-sign* with index *pro-index* in VAL licenses cases where a valent is controlled, as in the case of the subject

---

[20] There are also signs that appear on a predicator's ARG-ST list that do not appear on either the VAL or GAP list but rather are realized morphologically. For such signs Sag cites Miller and Monachesi (2003), the treatment of Romance pronominal "clitics" as verbal affixes, and we have no reason to revise that.

valent of the VP *go into a cup* in (52a), or the relativized valent in (52b). In these cases, the implicit argument and its overt counterpart sign are required to have the same discourse referent x. Similarly, the occurrence of a *covert-sign* argument with index *pro-index* in the third sublist of ARG-SG licenses understood imperative subjects, like (52c), for example. As already discussed in Section 2.3, these phenomena can co-occur, as in (52d). Null instantiation signs may appear only in the third sublist of ARG-ST, since (i) the definition of *construct* (50) requires all daughters to be overt signs and (ii) NI signs are by definition not controlled.

(52)   a.   I [made [the top]$_x$ [∅$_x$ go into a cup]].

     b.   This is the top$_x$ [that [∅$_x$ was damaged]].

     c.   ∅ Go to the last page.

     d.   Don't ∅$_i$ be so hard to please $\_\_j$.
        (Huddleston & Pullum, 2002, 1086)

The discourse referent variables of *pro-index* signs are unbound, and therefore not interpretable, but certain constructions, such as those in (52), bind the variables of *pro-index* arguments and allow them to be interpreted. The argument structure of a verb like *contribute*, specified as $\langle$ NP$_{x:\neg ni-index}$, NP$_{y:\neg dni-index}$, PP$_{z:\neg ini-index}$ $\rangle$, is consequently compatible with a total of 18 fully specified argument structures. For example, the subject can be resolved as *ref-index* (the subject is overtly realized) or *pro-index* (e.g. the subject is not realized, and is licit in controlled, imperative, or bare relative subject environments). Similarly the direct object can be resolved as *ref-index*, *pro-index*, or *ini-index*, and the oblique complement can be resolved as *ref-index*, *pro-index*, or *dni-index*. Any member of ARG-ST can be resolved a *pro-index*, since any argument can be relativized and extracted. See Section 3.5 for more details about extraction of implicit arguments in bare relative clauses.

    Item (53) is an illustrative lexical entry (listeme) for *contribute* that resolves to just the possibilities just discussed. We assume that frame arguments appear as the value of the list feature FES , instead of the usual features (e.g. a SITUATION (event variable) feature, and constituent features DONOR, GIFT, and RECIPIENT). This list encoding is chosen mainly as a convenient way to represent the linkage between ARG-ST members and the NI rules to be described later in this Element, though nothing hinges on this particular notational decision.[21]

---

[21] An alternative formulation would use variables over constituent features as in Koenig and Davis (2003).

(53)

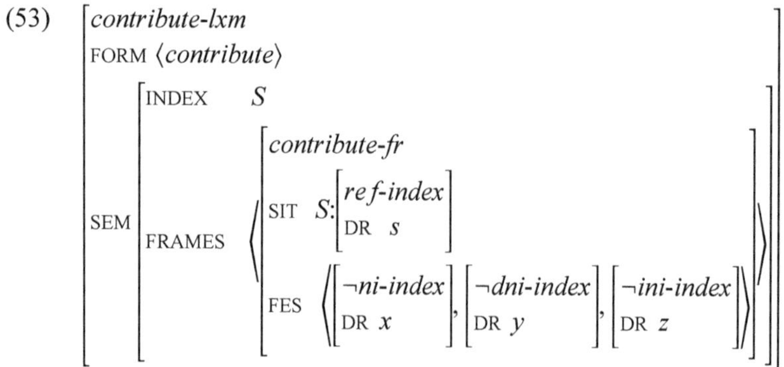

Thus, the *contribute-fr(ame)* is encoded as in predicate logic, as *contribute* (s,x,y,z), where s is a situation, x is the donor, y is the gift, and z is the recipient, respectively. None of these arguments can have expletive indices, since such indices bear no DR variables and are therefore uninterpretable. Since expletive indices are not felicitous members of FES, the subject constraint *¬ni-index* licenses either *ref-index* or *pro-index*; the direct object constraint *¬dni-index* licenses either *ref-index*, *ini-index*, or *pro-index*; and the indirect object constraint *¬ini-index* licences either *ref-index*, *dni-index*, or *pro-index*.[22]

Recall that the hierarchical lexicon is responsible for instantiating ARG-ST values in lexemes and for binding the indices in FRAMES to the appropriate arguments, as in (32), repeated here as (54), for prepositional transitive verbal lexemes like *contribute* in (53).

(54)
$$ptv\text{-}lxm \Rightarrow \begin{bmatrix} \text{ARG-ST} \left\langle \text{NP[\textsc{index} } X], \text{NP[\textsc{index} } Y], \text{PP[\textsc{index} } Z] \right\rangle \\ \text{SEM} \mid \text{FRAMES} \left\langle \begin{bmatrix} \text{FES } \langle X, Y, Z \rangle \end{bmatrix} \right\rangle \end{bmatrix}$$

Thus, the effect of the constraint in (54) is to instantiate the value of ARG-ST of all verbal lexemes that correspond to prepositional transitive verbs, or more techically, to resolve the underspecified value of ARG-ST for all lexemes typed as instances of *ptv-lxm*. In the case of the *contribute-lxm* sign in (53), this results in the lexeme shown in (55). The values of DR are made explicit here for exposition purposes. The result is a lexeme that selects a subject NP that must be overtly realized, a direct object that can be overt or INI, and an oblique object that can be overt or DNI.

---

[22] Since every argument of every lexeme has the possibility of a *pro-index*, in future representations of lexemes we will not show the *pro-index* option unless there is a specific reason to do so.

(55)
$$\begin{bmatrix} \textit{contribute-lxm} \\ \text{FORM } \langle \textit{contribute} \rangle \\ \text{SEM} \begin{bmatrix} \text{INDEX} \quad S \\ \text{FRAMES} \left\langle \begin{bmatrix} \textit{contribute-fr} \\ \text{SIT } \; S{:}\begin{bmatrix} \textit{ref-index} \\ \text{DR } s \end{bmatrix} \\ \text{FES } \left\langle X{:}\begin{bmatrix} \neg\textit{ni-index} \\ \text{DR } x \end{bmatrix}, Y{:}\begin{bmatrix} \neg\textit{dni-index} \\ \text{DR } y \end{bmatrix}, Z{:}\begin{bmatrix} \neg\textit{ini-index} \\ \text{DR } z \end{bmatrix} \right\rangle \end{bmatrix} \right\rangle \end{bmatrix} \\ \text{ARG-ST } \langle \text{NP[INDEX } X], \text{NP[INDEX } Y], \text{PP[INDEX } Z] \rangle \end{bmatrix}$$

Suppose that X resolves as *ref-index*, Y as *ini-index*, and Z as *dni-index*, and the lexeme undergoes past tense inflection. Then, the resulting *word* sign interacts with the ARP in (51) to make possible uses like (56a), by licensing signs like (56b). The subject NP *I* combines with the verb via the Subject-Predicate Construction in (42), and yields the clause (56b).

(56) a. I contributed Ø Ø. Didn't you?

   b.
$$\begin{bmatrix} \textit{word} \\ \text{FORM } \langle \textit{contributed} \rangle \\ \text{SYN} \begin{bmatrix} \text{CAT} \begin{bmatrix} \textit{verb} \\ \text{XARG} \quad K \\ \text{LID} \quad \langle L \rangle \end{bmatrix} \\ \text{VAL} \quad \langle K \rangle \\ \text{GAP} \quad \langle \, \rangle \end{bmatrix} \\ \text{SEM} \begin{bmatrix} \text{INDEX} \quad S \\ \text{FRAMES} \left\langle L : \begin{bmatrix} \textit{contribute-fr} \\ \text{SIT } \; S{:}\begin{bmatrix} \textit{ref-index} \\ \text{DR } s \end{bmatrix} \\ \text{FES } \left\langle X{:}\begin{bmatrix} \textit{ref-index} \\ \text{DR } x \end{bmatrix}, Y{:}\begin{bmatrix} \textit{ini-index} \\ \text{DR } y \end{bmatrix}, Z{:}\begin{bmatrix} \textit{dni-index} \\ \text{DR } z \end{bmatrix} \right\rangle \end{bmatrix}, \begin{bmatrix} \textit{past-fr} \\ \text{SIT } S \end{bmatrix} \right\rangle \end{bmatrix} \\ \text{ARG-ST } \langle K {:}\text{NP[INDEX } X], \text{NP[INDEX } Y], \text{PP[INDEX } Z] \rangle \end{bmatrix}$$

A derivation is shown in Figure 4, including the unary-branching step that inflects the verbal lexeme into the past tense word. The feature FRAMES is omitted for perspicuity.

If the subject is instead resolved as *pro-index*, it cannot then be discharged from VAL, because only canonical signs can appear in the feature DTRS.

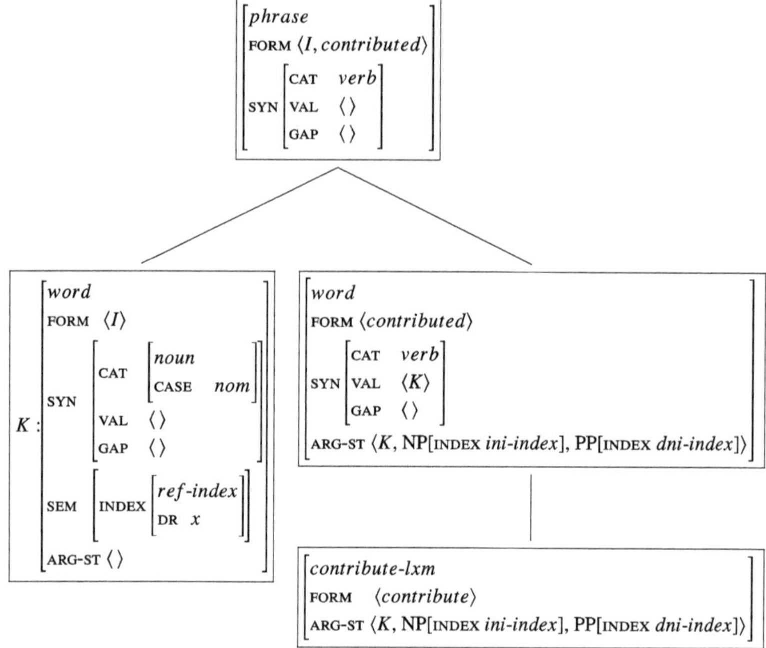

Figure 4 The clause *I contributed.*

However, a controller verb (or other predicating word) can select a VP with a *pro-index* subject and bind its discourse referent to that of its complement, as in (57). Although only DR values are bound, rather than INDEX values, we say that the two signs are *co-indexed,* in the traditional sense.

(57) a. I [made him$_x$ [∅$_x$ contribute ∅ ∅]].

  b. 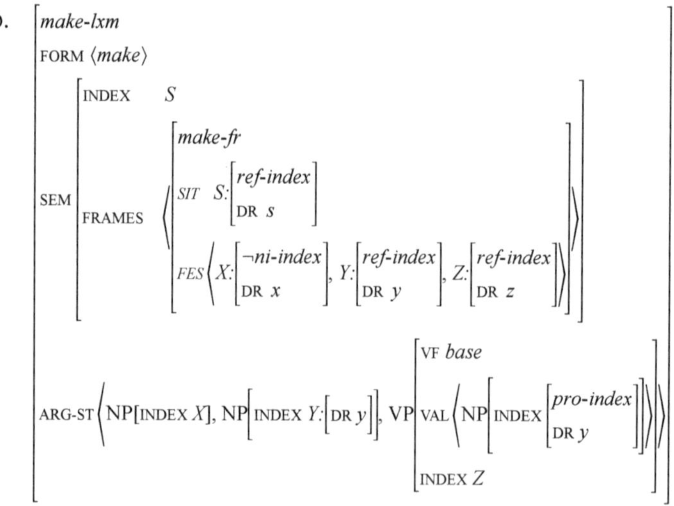

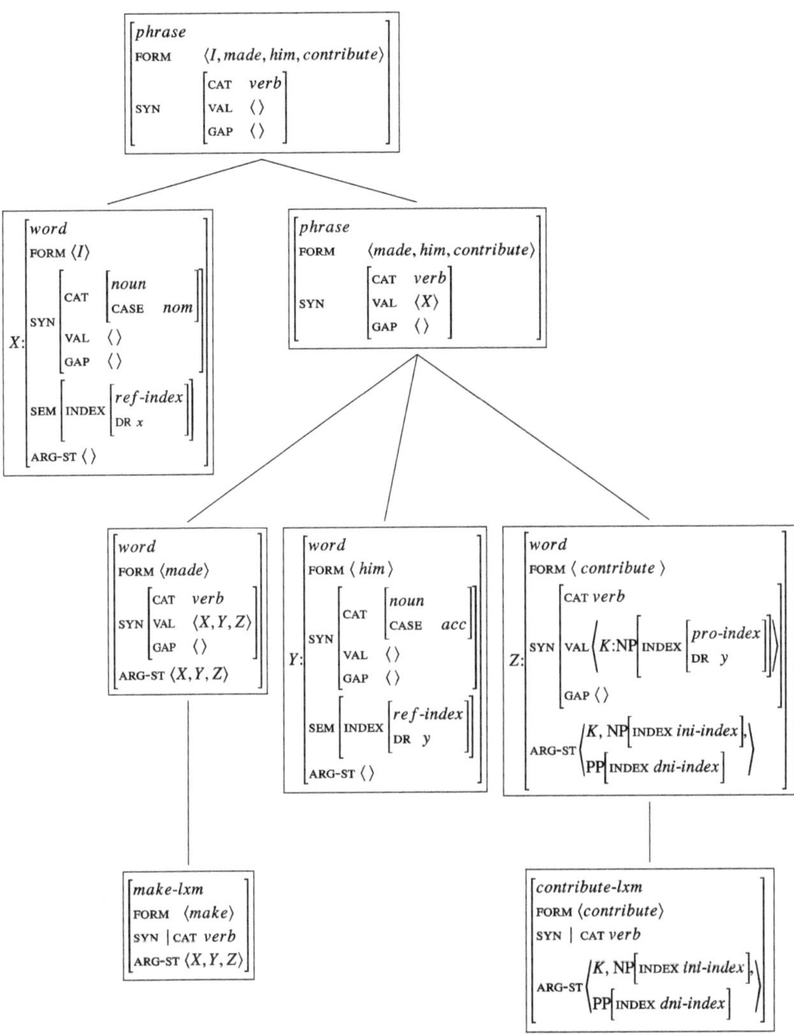

Figure 5 The clause *I made him contribute.*

The verb *make* ("cause") selects a subject, a direct object, and a base form VP. The unsaturated argument of the VP is *pro-index* and therefore has no PHON or FORM information, as a *covert-sign*. The discourse referent (DR) y of the unsaturated subject of the complement VP, however, is identified with *make*'s direct objects. The sentence in (57a) obtains the analysis in Figure 5, where *made* selects a direct object and binds its discourse referent y to that of the unsaturated valent of the VP *contribute*.

For resolutions where the direct object and/or the oblique object of *contribute* are resolved as bearing *ref-index* indices the result is essentially the same as above, except that now VAL is no longer a singleton list containing just the subject. Any complements resolved as *ref-index* are required by the ARP to appear in VAL (or GAP, as detailed in Section 3.5). In (58), both the subject and the direct object are referential and the oblique complement is resolved as DNI.

(58)   a.   I contributed something Ø. Didn't you?

b.

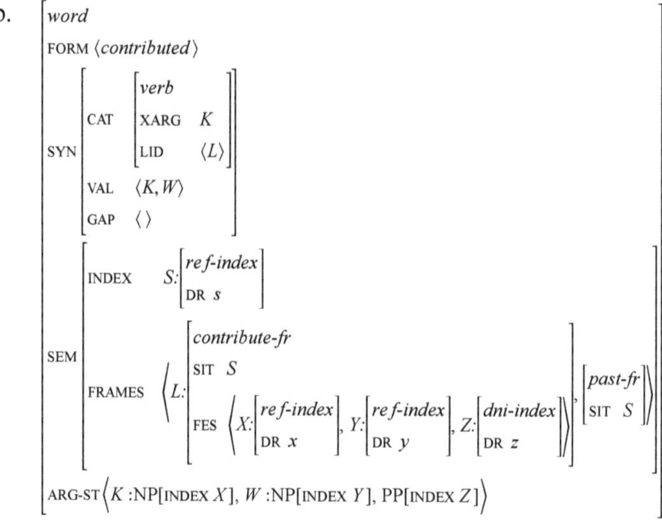

The complex VP *contributed something* is licensed by the application of the Predicational Head-Complement Construction in (41), discharging the complement NP W as a rightward sister of the verb. The remainder of the clause is licensed in the usual way, via the Subject-Predicate Construction in (42), which discharges the subject NP K from the VP's VAL list, as usual. The result is depicted in Figure 6.

In so-called arbitrary-pro constructions like (59), we assume that the XARG of the lexical verb (*err*) is resolved as *pro-index* and that a generic quantifier is added to the FRAMES list of that verb, binding the variable of the *pro-index* subject. All else proceeds as usual, according to independent principles. That is, the infinitive verb *to* selects a nonfinite VP complement and raises its subject as usual via the same structure-sharing mechanism already illustrated in Figure 5.

(59)   Ø To err is human.

3.3 NI Licensed by Context

We now turn to cases where features of the discourse context, including narrative context and shared background knowledge, allow a predicator to exhibit NI potential it does not possess inherently. As discussed, in a situation of sufficient immediacy and salience, an object that does not inherently license DNI may remain implicit. Attested examples of *Accessibility DNI* were given in (13), and a subset are reintroduced here as (60).

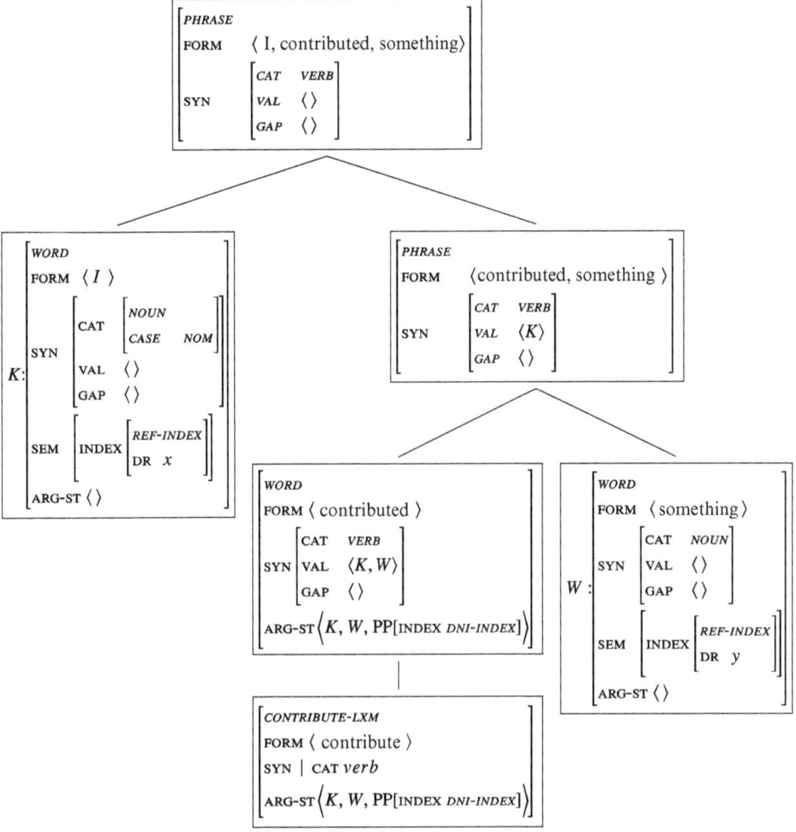

Figure 6 The clause *I contributed something.*

(60) a. I leaped to my feet and stumbled toward her. My fingers grabbed for the deadly necklace. I pulled Ø with all my strength. Snap! (Stine, undated)

  b. Suddenly the boulder was rocking and Tola Beg pushed Ø hard, pushed Ø with all the strength he had in his old body and with all the strength he had in his mind. (L'Amour, 2001, 36)

  c. @Announcer: And he's behind Lehtonen, 3 seconds left, Ø passes it to Sutton, and THE THRASHERS WIN 2–0.

We take the key concept at work in licensing this kind of NI to be the *accessibility* of an intended referent (Ariel, 2001; Gregory & Michaelis, 2001). As the name suggests, accessibility is conceived as a gradient property: the degree to which "the speaker can predict or could have predicted that a particular linguistic item will or would occur in a particular position within a sentence" (Prince, 1981a, 226). We posit that in any utterance context there is a threshold degree d

of accessibility such that when the degree of accessibility of a referent x denoted by a valent v equals or exceeds d, DNI is licensed for v. The ACCESSIBLE feature is therefore discrete: A referent is ACCESSIBLE *iff* its degree of accessibility equals or exceeds the threshold.[23] The ACCESSIBLE feature is posited to be one of the C(ONTEXTUAL) features (see Sag (2012, 96) and Pollard and Sag (1994, 332–335) for discussion of C-INDS).

The Accessibility DNI Construction is a derivational construction (mapping lexemes to other lexemes) that allows a valent with a sufficiently accessible referent in the context to be interpreted as DNI. Thus, the construction a lexeme and outputs an otherwise identical lexeme in which the accessible valent is interpreted as DNI. The Accessibility DNI Construction is formalized in (61). The paired tags X and $X!$ notate the fact that the values of MTR and DTRS are the same in all respects other than those that are explicitly shown to differ, as discussed in connection with (41).[24] Thus, MTR and DTR have the same values for FORM and SYN, and differ only relative to SEM: One of the semantic arguments, Y, typed as *ref-index* in DTR, is now typed as *dni-index* in the mother node. Its DR variable remains the same x, nonetheless.

(61)   **Accessibility DNI Construction** ($\uparrow$*derivational-cxt*)
accessible-dni-cxt $\Rightarrow$

$$
\begin{bmatrix}
\text{MTR } X! \begin{bmatrix}
\text{SEM} \begin{bmatrix} \text{FRAMES} \left\langle \begin{bmatrix} \text{FES} \quad L_1 \oplus \left\langle Y! \begin{bmatrix} \textit{dni-index} \end{bmatrix} \right\rangle \oplus L_2 \end{bmatrix}, \ldots \right\rangle \end{bmatrix} \\[2ex]
\text{CNTXT} \begin{bmatrix} \text{ACCESSIBLE } x \end{bmatrix}
\end{bmatrix} \\[3ex]
\text{DTRS} \left\langle X: \begin{bmatrix} \text{SEM} \begin{bmatrix} \text{FRAMES} \left\langle \begin{bmatrix} \text{FES} \quad L_1 \oplus \left\langle Y: \begin{bmatrix} \textit{ref-index} \\ \text{DR } x \end{bmatrix} \right\rangle \oplus L_2 \end{bmatrix}, \ldots \right\rangle \end{bmatrix} \end{bmatrix} \right\rangle
\end{bmatrix}
$$

The ACCESSIBLE feature normally takes the value *none*, but in this construction it is required to take a variable of one of the referential arguments, indicating the accessibility of the intended referent x is at or above threshold. The first frame in FRAMES is the main predication (the root of the embedding tree of

---

[23] We leave to future research the question whether the threshold of accessibility varies with utterance context or is in some sense constant. Also, it is an open question whether accessibility is in fact observable independently of its inferred effect on utterances.

[24] Ideally, (61) would state that the ARG-ST values of the mother and daughter are not identical, but since this is ensured by the index type change in FRAMES, and thus predictable, we refrain from explicitly stating the ARG-ST values, to keep this and subsequent derivational NI constructions as readable as possible.

frames discussed in the text introducing the LID in [35]), so this is the only frame that needs to be altered by (61). As indicated by the ellipses ..., any such other frames remain unaltered by our NI lexical rules.

Recall that ARG-ST constraints like (54) apply to lexemes, which means that they apply to both the daughter and the mother of (61). Thus, the value of ARG-ST of the mother node is resolved as a list of valents, the indices of which are bound to the respective frame elements in FES. Thus, on the daughter's ARG-ST list the accessible sign will have a *ref-index*, while on the mother's ARG-ST list this otherwise identical sign has a *dni-index*. Both signs have the same [DR x] specification, since only the index type is altered by (61). An application of a construct licensed by (61) is illustrated in Figure 7, in tree format. The daughter node of Figure 7 corresponds to the sign in DTRS in (61) and the mother node is a sign that corresponds to the value of MTR.

Although the object of *pull* is listemically typed as *ref-index*, and therefore unable to be null instantiated, the construction in (61) can override this provided that its referent x is deemed accessible in the given context.[25] The general constraint for the ARG-ST of simple transitive verbs, shown in (62), ensures the ARG-ST value is properly instantiated, for both uses of *pull* seen in Figure 7.

$$(62) \quad STV\text{-}LXM \Rightarrow \begin{bmatrix} \text{ARG-ST} \left\langle \text{XP}[\text{INDEX } X], \text{NP}[\text{INDEX } Y] \right\rangle \\ \text{SEM} \mid \text{FRAMES} \left\langle \begin{bmatrix} \text{FES } \langle X, Y \rangle \end{bmatrix}, ... \right\rangle \end{bmatrix}$$

We now turn our attention to *dispositional NI*. As already noted, Ruppenhofer and Michaelis (2010) point out that generic, including habitual, aspect can license indefinite null instantiation of the direct object of a simple transitive verb, such as *arrest*, while this is not possible under other circumstances, as illustrated in (15), repeated here as (63) for convenience. See also Mittwoch (2005) for related discussion.

(63) a. * The cops arrested Ø last night.
       (Ruppenhofer & Michaelis, 2010, 159)

   b. Sure, the cops arrest Ø when they can, but it's always in small amounts.
       (Ruppenhofer & Michaelis, 2010, 159)

---

[25] The object of *pull* may also be resolved as *pro-index*, since every argument may be listemically so typed, but we will in future tacitly assume this in the text, as we have been doing in the AVMs. Technically, it is not *ref-index* that is overridden, but the disjunction *ref-index* ∨ *pro-index*.

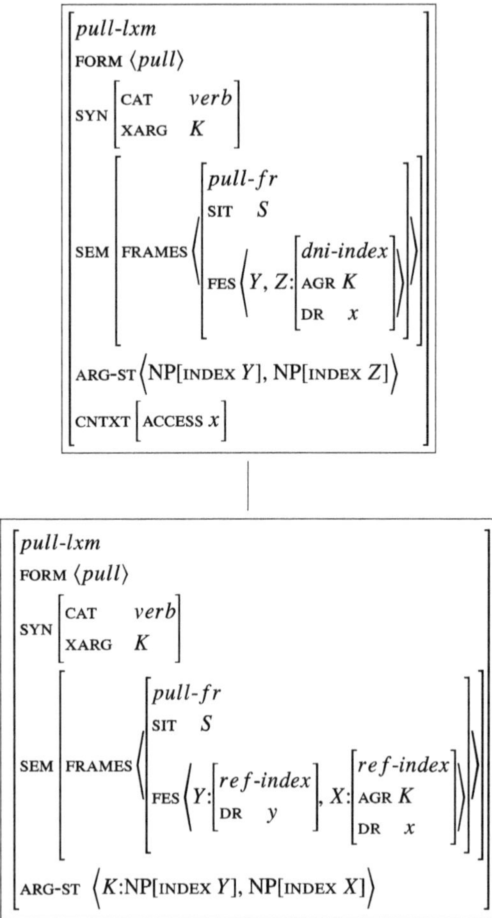

Figure 7 Accessibility DNI construction applied to the internal argument of the verb *pull*.

Even a strongly anti-NI verb like *devour* will allow object INI in dispositional contexts:

(64) Once Ragnarök is triggered, it will devour Ø until it has destroyed the last of this world. (Flowers, 2018)

Boneh (2019) proposes a stativizing *dispositional* operator that may yield habitual, generic, or disposition readings depending on circumstances. Null complementation licensing habitual interpretation as exemplified above is restricted to a non-quantificational existence interpretation, INI (Ruppenhofer & Michaelis, 2010, 164) , and is also restricted to non-subjects. We model these facts in the dispositional INI construction, shown in (65).

(65) **Dispositional INI Construction** ($\uparrow$ *derivational-cxt*)

dispositional-ini-cxt $\Rightarrow$

$$
\begin{bmatrix}
\text{MTR } X!\begin{bmatrix} \text{SEM} \begin{bmatrix} \text{FRAMES} \left\langle \begin{bmatrix} \text{FES } L_1 \oplus \langle\, \textit{ini-index}\, \rangle \oplus L_2 \end{bmatrix}, \begin{bmatrix} \textit{dispositional-fr} \\ \text{SIT} \quad S \end{bmatrix} \right\rangle \oplus L_3 \end{bmatrix} \end{bmatrix} \\[2em]
\text{DTRS } \left\langle X\!: \begin{bmatrix} \text{SEM} \begin{bmatrix} \text{INDEX } S \\ \text{FRAMES} \left\langle \begin{bmatrix} \text{FES } L_1\!:\!\textit{ne-list} \oplus \langle\, \textit{ref-index}\, \rangle \oplus L_2 \end{bmatrix} \right\rangle \oplus L_3 \end{bmatrix} \end{bmatrix} \right\rangle
\end{bmatrix}
$$

In (65), a nonsubject argument typed as *ref-index* is selected to become *ini-index*, regardless of the initial lexemic specification. We can ensure that the argument in question is not a subject because we assume that frame elements appear in order, in all English verbal listemes, such that the first frame element always corresponds to the external argument. The constraint [FES L_1:*ne-list* $\oplus\langle$ *ref-index* $\rangle \oplus L_2$], states that the list value of FES of the verb frame is split into three sublists: one non-empty L_1 sublist (which contains the referent of the subject), a singleton sublist containing a *ref-index* frame element, and a third sublist L_2 (which may or not be empty). As before, the value of ARG-ST of the mother node is underspecified and resolved via the linking rules that are appropriate given the lexeme type that is fed into the rule. As a result, a referential index is turned into a INI index, but its DR variable remains the same.

The change to a *ini-index* index, which is a noncanonical index, forces the sign bearing it to become *covert-sign*, according to (49). The mother's FRAMES list contains a *dispositional-fr*(*ame*), representing a stativizing operator that takes an event argument and subsumes a quasi-universal operator over instances of a kind (Boneh, 2019). The analysis is shown in Figure 8. We from now on omit the SYN values from the derivation examples for exposition purposes, as they remain unchanged by NI constructions.

Sentences like those in (66) have the look of counterexamples to the Boneh formulation of disposition, since they refer to a single episode. We note, however, that in each case a disposition to kill is presupposed or entailed. Dispositional INI is apparently sensitive to dispositions involved in an utterance that need not be asserted.

(66) a. [@]Once a bear has killed, it automatically earns the death penalty, as bears are creatures of habit and will get in trouble with humans again.

  b. [@]Once a dog has killed there is no going back, there's no "training" for this, she's tasted blood.

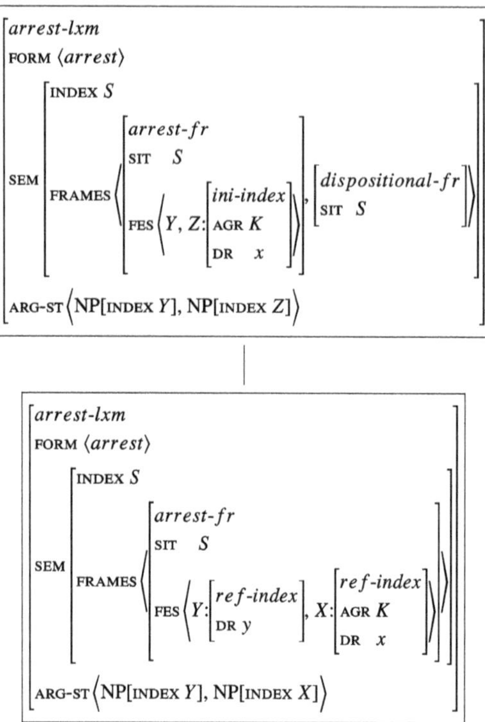

Figure 8 Dispositional INI construction as applied to the verb *arrest*.

c. @Once a dog has killed it is likely to kill again …

d. @I think it harks back to the old beliefs like once a dog has killed it will seek to do it again and again – the bloodlust theory.

3.4 NI Licensed by Genre

As already noted, Ruppenhofer and Michaelis (2010) show there are at least five distinct genres that license NI: instructional imperative, "labelese," diary style, sports reporting ("match reports"), and certain nonquotative verbs used quotatively. See Ruppenhofer and Michaelis (2010, 160) for examples. Two examples of context-induced DNI illustrate what Ruppenhofer and Michaelis (2010) term *labelese* – for example, (67a), and the diary genre – for example, (67b). For all five genres NI is of the deictic/anaphoric – that is, DNI, variety and, in some cases, targets erstwhile subjects.

(67)   a.   Ø Contains alcohol.

   (Ruppenhofer & Michaelis, 2010, 160)

b. Ø Read Michelet; Ø wrote to Desmond about his poetess; ... Ø played gramophone...

(Ruppenhofer & Michaelis, 2010, 160)

Ruppenhofer and Michaelis (2010) note that diary genre DNI involves the definite interpretation of an unrealized first-person subject that is necessarily a topic, and propose a phrasal construction for diary genre DNI to license examples like those in (18). Here, we remain with the lexical approach, as shown in (68), and view the accessibility of the author as entailed by the genre itself.

(68) **Diary Genre DNI Construction** ($\uparrow$ *derivational-cxt*)

$$\textit{diary-dni-cxt} \Rightarrow$$

$$\begin{bmatrix} \text{MTR } X! \begin{bmatrix} \text{SEM} \begin{bmatrix} \text{FRAMES} \left\langle \begin{bmatrix} \text{FES } \langle \textit{dni-index} \rangle \oplus L \end{bmatrix}, ... \right\rangle \end{bmatrix} \\[2ex] \text{CNTXT} \begin{bmatrix} \text{C-INDS} \begin{bmatrix} \text{TOPIC } x \\ \text{GENRE } \textit{diary} \end{bmatrix} \end{bmatrix} \end{bmatrix} \\[4ex] \text{DTRS} \left\langle X\!: \begin{bmatrix} \text{SEM} \begin{bmatrix} \text{FRAMES} \left\langle \begin{bmatrix} \text{FES} \left\langle \begin{bmatrix} \textit{ref-index} \\ \text{AGR} \begin{bmatrix} \text{PER} & 1\textit{st} \\ \text{NUM} & \textit{sg} \end{bmatrix} \\ \text{DR } x \end{bmatrix} \right\rangle \oplus L \end{bmatrix}, ... \right\rangle \end{bmatrix} \end{bmatrix} \right\rangle \end{bmatrix}$$

In construction (68), the CNTXT value constrains TOPIC and GENRE features. The GENRE value is *diary* and the TOPIC value is identified with the subject referent x. The mother's value differs from that of the daughter in that the subject's index is *ref-index* in the daughter and *dni-index* in the mother, as in Figure 9. The frame element typed *dni-index* in MTR retains all the information it has in DTRS, including AGR and DR.

The labelese genre consists of structures describing generic properties of provenance and purpose of the item in question, as illustrated in (67a) and (69).

(69) a. Ø Processed in a facility that processes tree nuts.

b. Ø Manufactured using equipment that processes shellfish.

c. Ø Gives long-lasting shine Ø .

Our account of the labelese construction is very similar to that of the diary genre, as seen in (70). A referential subject is recast as DNI and the construction is only appropriate in a particular kind of context. Further constraints on FRAMES are necessary, requiring that x denote a (manufactured or agricultural) product

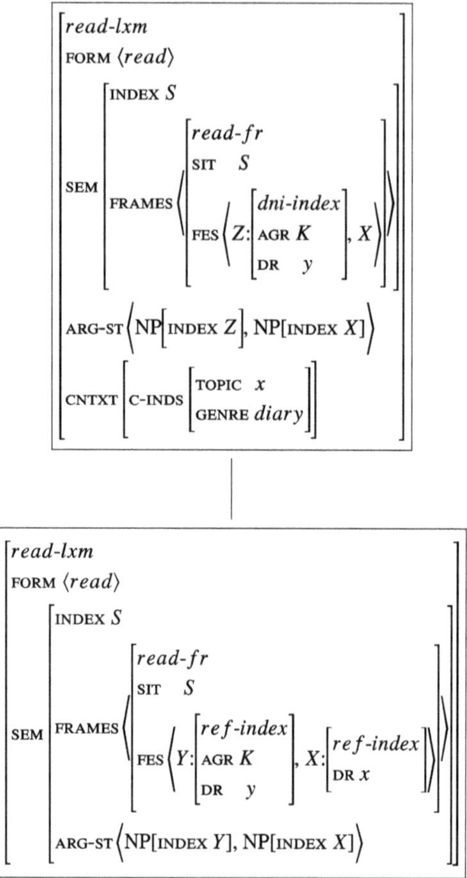

Figure 9 Diary genre DNI construction as applied to the verb *read*.

with a given purpose. This could be effected by appending *product(x)* to the value of FRAMES in the mother node of (70).

(70)   **Labelese Genre DNI Construction** (↑ *derivational-cxt*)

We now turn our attention to instructional imperatives, but in order to do so, we need to settle on an account of imperative constructions. As is well known, imperative constructions allow the omission of a second-person subject, as an implicit addressee, which is assigned the same semantic content for the understood subject as the pronoun *you*. Sag et al. (2003) propose to account for imperatives with a (nonheaded) phrasal rule that projects a finite S node from a nonfinite VP daughter. Such a rule is nonheaded because the verb form feature (encoded as a head feature) of the daughter is inconsistent with that of the mother. But this difference suggests instead that the imperative should be a derivational lexical rule. We therefore assume that imperatives are obtained via a derivational rule whose daughter is a base form lexeme and whose mother is a morphologically a plain-form (Huddleston and Pullum 2002, 83, [CGEL]) verb, whose XARG appears on neither the VAL nor GAP lists and is interpreted like a second-person pronoun, as formalized in (71).

(71)　**Imperative Construction** (↑ *derivational-cxt*)

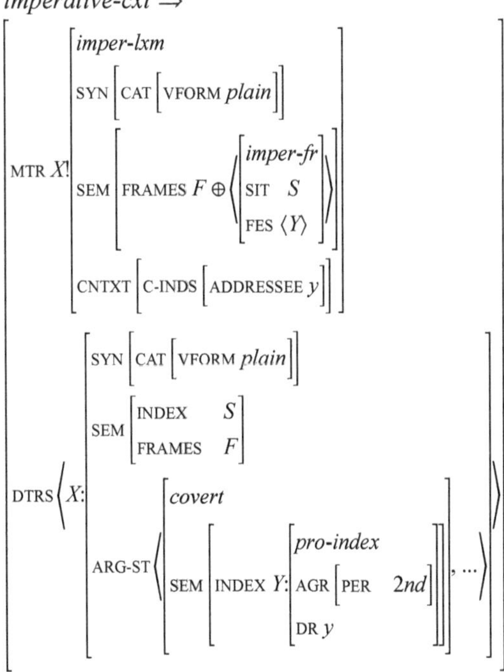

In (71), the subject is required to be resolved as a covert *pro-index* sign. Such a resolution was a possibility all along, since external arguments in listemes generally have the *pro-index* option and do not cause a problem so long as they are given an interpretation, for example, in control environments, as already discussed. The definition of construct in (50) prevents the subject from being realized overtly because of its INDEX type, but it remains available on the ARG-ST to bind an anaphor if necessary, as in (72).[26]

(72) $\emptyset_x$ Protect yourself$_x$ from 5G.

We assume imperative semantics consists in a relation between an individual Y (the understood second person subject) and a state of affairs S, as indicated in the mother's FRAMES in (71). Other possibilities exist. The application of the rule in (71) is illustrated in Figure 10.

Recall that we define a root clause as any verbal sign with empty VAL and GAP specifications, as seen in (43). The verbal lexemes licensed by the imperative construction can satisfy such a constraint because the ARP allows *pro-index* covert signs to be absent from VAL and GAP. Thus, we get structures like the one in Figure 11.

We are now in a position to address the instructional imperative. This construction is of interest because, along with DNI suppression of a nonsubject argument, it includes the familiar unexpressed second-person subject of imperatives, as in (73).

(73)   a.   Method: Blend all the ingredients in an electric blender. Serve $\emptyset$ cold.
             (Ruppenhofer & Michaelis, 2010, 106)

        b.   Chill $\emptyset$ before serving $\emptyset$.
             (Ruppenhofer & Michaelis, 2010, 159)

        c.   In a bowl, toss $\emptyset$ with salt and set $\emptyset$ aside.
             (Ruppenhofer & Michaelis, 2014, 72)

        d.   In a skillet, sauté $\emptyset$ until browned but not crisp.
             (Ruppenhofer & Michaelis, 2014, 72)

Although Bender (1999) and Ruppenhofer and Michaelis (2010) propose a phrasal construction, we continue here to pursue a lexical approach, treating these phenomena as licensed by derivational lexical constructions. We analyze the uses of the verbs verbs *chill* and *serve* in (73) via the instructional imperative construction, formalized in (74). Here, the daughter is an imperative verb lexeme – that is, the output (MTR) of the imperative construction in (71).

---

[26] See Pollard and Sag (1994, ch. 6) and Sag et al. (2003, ch. 7) for a purely lexical binding theory, stated at the level of ARG-ST, requiring that reflexive pronouns be co-referential with signs that precede them in the same ARG-ST list.

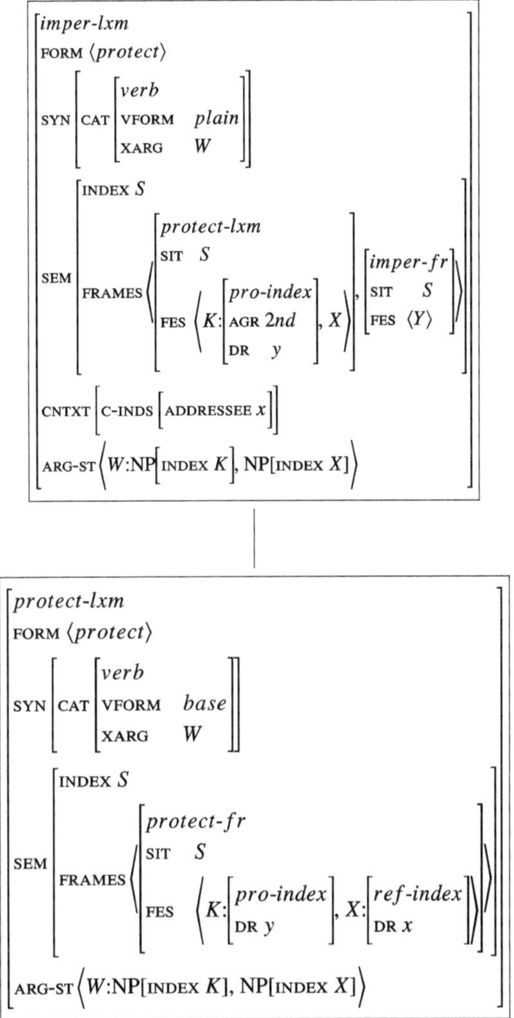

Figure 10 Derivation of the imperative form for *protect* in (72).

(74)   **Instructional Imperative DNI Construction** ($\uparrow$*derivational-cxt*)

instructional-imperative-dni-cxt $\Rightarrow$

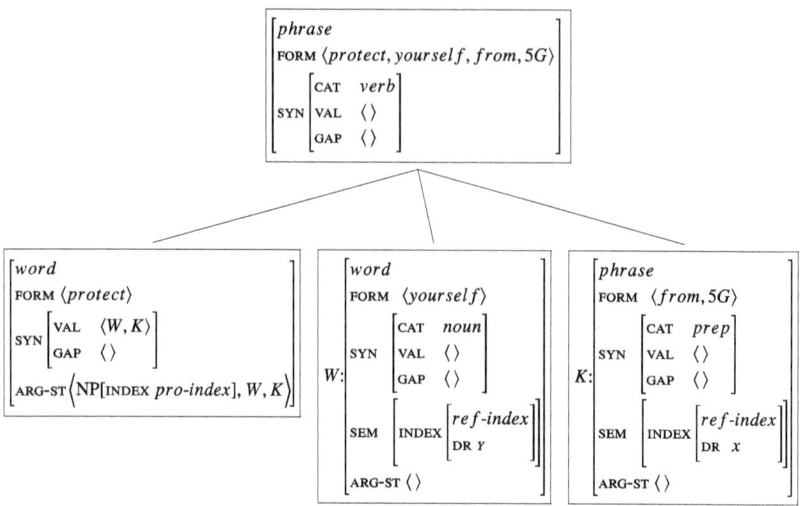

Figure 11 The clause *Protect yourself from 5G!* (abbreviated).

The MTR in the instructional imperative construction retains the characteristics of an imperative verb word that contains a referential nonsubject argument while replacing the index of that argument with *dni-index*.

Specifically, in the instructional imperative construction (71); (i) there is a pair of non-XARG ARG-ST members distributed across mother and daughter that are alike in having [DR x] in their INDEX but differ in their INDEX type, (ii) in the daughter's ARG-ST, the INDEX type of the [DR x] argument is *ref-index* while that in the mother's ARG-ST is *dni-index*, (iii) the x variable is contextually specified to be a TOPIC and (iv) the GENRE is contextually specified to be *instruction(al)*. The analysis is illustrated in Figure 12.[27]

3.5 Implicit Arguments and Displacement

Not all extraction requires a filler phrase, and thus in some cases the missing argument is simply missing, although it can be co-indexed with another implicit

---

[27] Another construction type that seems to involve an implicit subject is illustrated in (i–iv), which show that the missing subject is not restricted to any person, and is accessible to tag questions. Kay (2002) notes that these patterns could be due to a special construction for subject NI, or result from a pragmatically controlled form of sentence-initial ellipsis (e.g. as in *Ever heard of a phone?* and *Took him long enough to propose*). The evidence is mixed, and we leave this matter unresolved due to space limitations.

   i. Blew it, didn't I/you?
   ii. Fooled you/us (, didn't they/she).
   iii. Got it.
   iv. Found it.

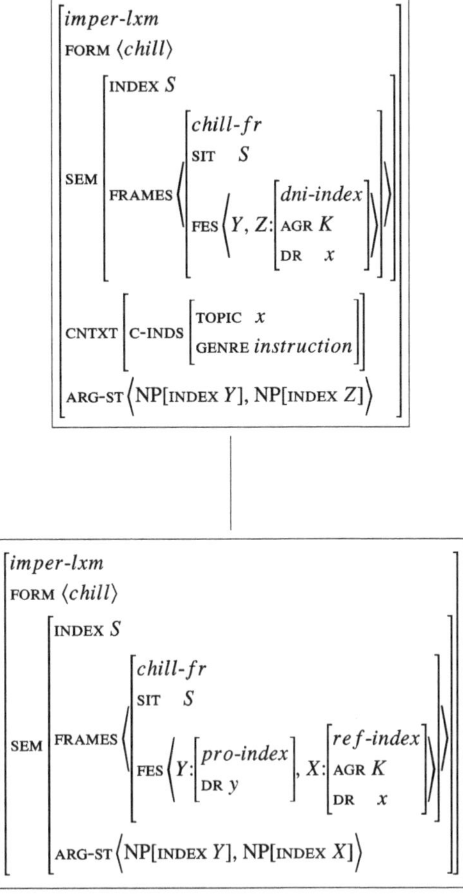

Figure 12 Instructional imperative DNI construction as applied to the verb *chill*.

phrase. In examples (75a) and (75b), the reference of the implicit subject is constructionally controlled, and therefore best seen as *pro*.

(75) a. Don't $\emptyset_x$ be so hard to get $\_x$, baby.
          [Rick James, *You and I*]

   b. $\emptyset_x$ Being especially easy to talk to $\_x$, Pat$_x$ was set to become a great therapist.

In the case of (75a), the extracted theme is required to be the imperative subject (i.e. a second-person nominal who is the addressee), whereas in (75b), the dangling participle construction independently requires the external argument of the prepended phrase to be co-referential with the external argument of the matrix clause. This contrasts with NI, whereby context determines the reference of the implicit arguments rather than a controller introduced by the construction.

Sag (2012) adopts a feature-based approach to argument realization in which members of ARG-ST are allowed to appear either in VAL(ence) or in GAP. Members of ARG-ST that appear in GAP are percolated in syntactic structure to license potentially long-distance dependencies, whereas those members of ARG-ST that appear in VAL must be locally realized. However, Sag (2012) is not entirely clear about how members of ARG-ST are related to VAL and GAP, in particular, how subjects are mapped into GAP.[28] Moreover, the PHCC in (41) forces the external argument to always be on the VAL list, which in turn incorrectly prevents subject extraction in VPs. We therefore revise the PHCC as seen in (76).

(76)   **Predicational Head-Complement Construction** ($\uparrow$*headed-cxt*) [revised]

$$\textit{pred-hd-comp-cxt} \Rightarrow$$

$$\begin{bmatrix} \text{MTR} & \begin{bmatrix} \text{SYN } X! \begin{bmatrix} \text{VAL L1} \end{bmatrix} \end{bmatrix} \\ \text{DTRS} & \langle Z \rangle \oplus L_2 \text{: } \textit{ne-list} \\ \text{HD-DTR } Z\text{:} & \begin{bmatrix} \textit{word} \\ \text{SYN } X : \begin{bmatrix} \text{CAT} \begin{bmatrix} \text{XARG } Y \end{bmatrix} \\ \text{VAL } L_1 : \langle (Y) \rangle \oplus L_2 : \textit{list}(\neg Y) \end{bmatrix} \end{bmatrix} \end{bmatrix}$$

Recall that the ARP in (51) allows any member of ARG-ST (including the XARG) to appear on either the VAL list or on the GAP list. The version of the PHCC in (76) interacts with the ARP to allow any argument (including the external argument) to be overtly realized (locally or nonlocally). This is possible because the VAL list of the head daughter is the concatenation "$\oplus$" of two sublists: L_1 and L_2. The first list L_1 must (at most) contain the XARG (the parenthesis around Y in $\langle (Y) \rangle$ express optionality), and the latter list L_2 is required to be non-empty and prohibited from containing the XARG (i.e. the parametric type $\textit{list}(\neg Y)$ states that none of the members of the list L_2 can unify with Y). Thus, if the XARG is in VAL, then that subject phrase is realized locally, and if instead the XARG appears on the GAP list, then the phrase has been extracted.

 Sag (2012) cites the Ginzburg and Sag (2000) analysis, which accounts for subject extraction via a different mechanism from that of object extraction, but in the light of Levine & Hukari (2006, 87–109), extraction of subjects and complements should be handled uniformly.

We can now turn to the problem of modeling the interaction between displacement and implicit arguments. Our grammar predicts the acceptability of *pro* in missing object constructions such as (75), repeated as (77), without further stipulation.

(77)   a.   Don't $\emptyset_x$ be so hard to please $\_\_x$.
             (Huddleston & Pullum, 2002, 1086)

       b. $\emptyset_x$ Being especially easy to talk to $\_\_x$, Pat was set to become a great therapist.

Signs that are of the sort *pro-index* are not allowed in DTRS because the definition of construct in (50) requires daughters to be overt signs, but they are allowed in GAP. This predicts that the object of *please* in (77a) can be typed *pro-index* and appear in GAP. The sign is percolated in the sentence structure like any other extracted sign, and is instantiated with the external argument of the adjective *hard* as in Figure 13.

The subject X of the adjective is raised like any other subject all the way to the VP selected by the auxiliary verb. At this point, the DR of the remaining valent in the VP VAL list is instantiated with the external argument of the auxiliary. In this case, the verb is in imperative mood, and therefore its understood subject is also *pro-index*, as required by the imperative construction. The same analysis applies to (77b). In bare relatives like (78a) an analogous situation arises: the extracted *pro* argument is percolated via GAP, and the construction itself links its DR to the head of the relative, binding it, via a general construction (approximately) of the form $N_x \rightarrow N_x$ S[GAP $\langle NP_x[\text{INDEX } pro\text{-}index]\rangle$]; see Sag (1997) and Sag (2010). Thus, although the implicit argument is a gap, the clause is licit because the sign is discharged from the GAP list. The same applies to most non-*wh*-relative constructions, including *for* infinitival relatives like (78b), and *to* infinitival relatives like (78c).

(78)   a.   The book$_x$ [(that) I want you to read $\_\_x$] is this one.

       b.   Sam found a person$_x$ [for you to talk to $\_\_x$].

       c.   The next contestant$_x$ [$\_\_x$ to answer the question correctly] will get bonus points.

Conversely, the present account predicts that examples like (79) are illicit. No type of covert sign is allowed in DTRS, and thus there is no way to discharge a covert sign in GAP and saturate the root sign. Recall that all root signs must be verbal, finite, and bear empty VAL and GAP specifications (Ginzburg & Sag, 2000, 45).

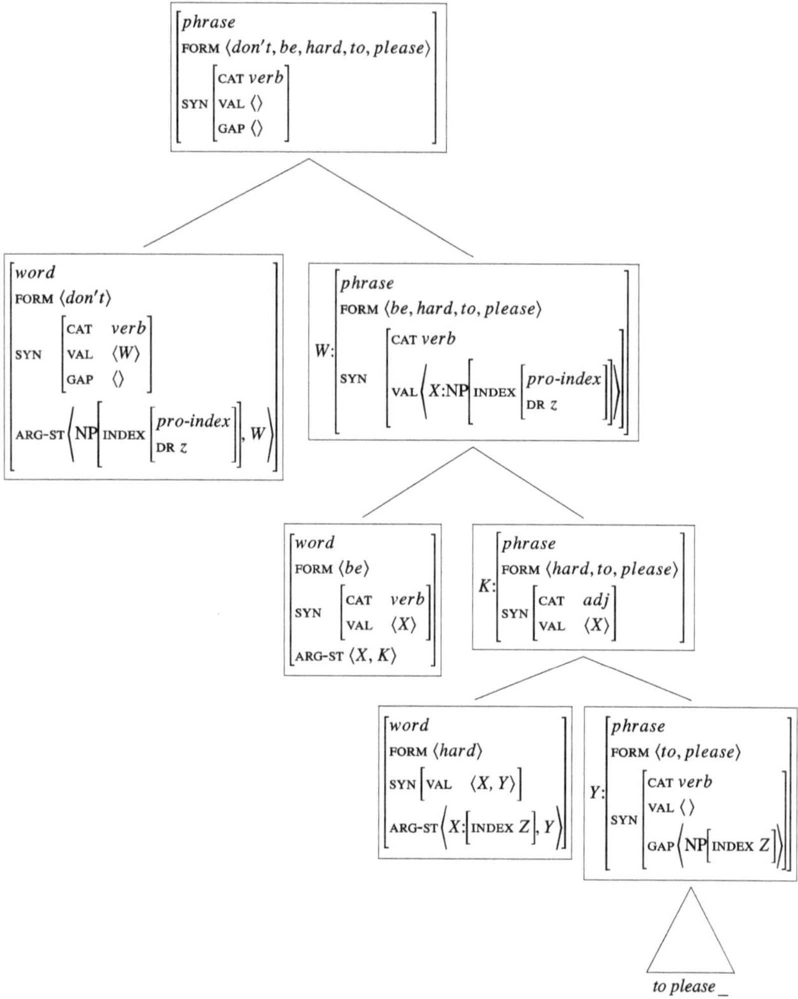

Figure 13 Percolation of a gap into an understood external argument in a missing object construction.

(79) a. *∅$_x$ Do you think is easy to talk to _$_x$?
      (cf. 'Who$_x$ do you think is easy to talk to _$_x$?')

  b. *∅$_x$ I don't think I've met _$_x$.
      (cf. 'THAT GUY$_x$ I don't think I've met _$_x$.')

Let us now turn to the passivization of implicit arguments like (80). Such cases are likewise predicted without stipulations. In (80a), the NI direct object has been promoted to a passive subject. As usual, we assume that the lexical rule for passivization promotes the direct object to subject, and so the first member of ARG-ST of the passive form *fed* in (80a) is the *ni-index* theme. The example in (80b) has the extra complication that the passive subject is co-indexed with the prepositional object. The passive rule interacts with the grammar of missing object constructions to identify the extracted complement with the first member of ARG-SG of *take*.

(80)   a.   If $\emptyset_x$ properly fed $\_x$, iguanas can live for a long time.

       b.   If $\emptyset_x$ taken good care of $\_x$, iguanas can live for a long time.

Extant accounts of the passive such as Pollard and Sag (1994, 83), Boeckx (1998), and Bresnan (2001, 26), offer no principled (semantic/pragmatic) account of the optionality of the PP. Usually, the by-phrase is simply assumed to be optional. In this Element, we seek to ground this optionality in the cognitive status of the demoted agent. There are clear cases of INI interpretation of short passives such as (81).

(81)   a.   [@]I heard that they had been killed $\emptyset$, but no one knew who did it.

       b.   Two of them were shot by the demonstrators and another person was killed $\emptyset$, but no one knows by whom.

There are also cases like (82), which have suggested DNI to Fillmore and some later writers (see Lyngfeld (2012) for discussion and a third point of view). There appears to be an equally good case to be made for attributing the definite-seeming reading arising from cases like those in (82) to existential semantics strengthened by pragmatic inference. Guided by the principle of claiming no more for semantics per se than necessary, we model the semantics of short passive agents as INI.

(82)   a.   [@]"Have those teeth been brushed this year $\emptyset$?" Adella asked ..."I know I
             brushed mine in April for my birthday!" quipped the younger ...

       b.   [@]Only after the gloves have been removed $\emptyset$, the hands have been washed $\emptyset$, the patient has been dismissed $\emptyset$, and the area has been cleaned $\emptyset$, should the dental radiographer carry the disposable container holding the contaminated films to the darkroom.

We propose to model both long and short passives with the lexical rule in (83). The daughter must subcategorize an overt subject argument and at least one object, Y. The passive counterpart must have the appropriate inflection, via the ancillary morphological function f_{pass}. In the mother node, the object Y is now the subject, as it is the first element in ARG-ST. If the PP at the end of the ARG-ST is resolved as an overt sign, we obtain a long passive. If the PP is resolved as a covert sign, we obtain a short passive. Recall that covert signs are allowed in VAL in our ARP, but they cannot be discharged because only *overt-sign*s can appear in DTRS.[29]

(83)   **Passive Construction** ($\uparrow$*inflectional-cxt*)

$$\textit{passive-cxt} \Rightarrow$$

$$
\begin{bmatrix}
\text{MTR} & \begin{bmatrix}
\text{PHON } f_{pass}(L_3) \\[4pt]
\text{SYN} & \begin{bmatrix} \text{CAT} & \begin{bmatrix} \text{VFORM} & \textit{pass} \\ \text{XARG} & Y \end{bmatrix} \end{bmatrix} \\[10pt]
\text{SEM} & Z! \begin{bmatrix} \text{FRAMES} \left\langle \begin{bmatrix} \text{FES } \langle W \rangle \oplus L_2 \end{bmatrix} \right\rangle \end{bmatrix} \\[10pt]
\text{ARG-ST} & \langle Y \rangle \oplus L_1 \oplus \left\langle \text{PP} \begin{bmatrix} \text{MRKG } \textit{by} \\ \text{SEM} \begin{bmatrix} \text{INDEX } W : \begin{bmatrix} \textit{ini-index} \vee \textit{ref-index} \\ \text{DR} \quad x \end{bmatrix} \end{bmatrix} \end{bmatrix} \right\rangle
\end{bmatrix} \\[40pt]
\text{DTRS} & \left\langle \begin{bmatrix}
\text{PHON} & L_3 \\[4pt]
\text{SYN} & \begin{bmatrix} \text{CAT} \begin{bmatrix} \text{VFORM} & \textit{base} \end{bmatrix} \end{bmatrix} \\[8pt]
\text{SEM} & Z : \begin{bmatrix} \text{FRAMES} \left\langle \begin{bmatrix} \text{FES } \langle X \rangle \oplus L_2 \end{bmatrix} \right\rangle \end{bmatrix} \\[10pt]
\text{ARG-ST} & \left\langle \begin{bmatrix} \textit{overt-sign} \\ \text{SEM} \begin{bmatrix} \text{INDEX } X : \begin{bmatrix} \textit{ref-index} \\ \text{DR} \quad x \end{bmatrix} \end{bmatrix} \end{bmatrix} \right\rangle \oplus \langle Y \rangle \oplus L_1
\end{bmatrix} \right\rangle
\end{bmatrix}
$$

The subject and XARG of the passive form of a transitive verb will be the second member of the daughter's ARG-ST, here Y, as a consequence of the constraint in (45), which states that the first member of ARG-ST is structure-shared with XARG. The XARG variable x is now linked to the PP argument. As usual, the ARP in

---

[29] The NI patterns licensed by the *Way* Construction, briefly discussed in Section 1, amount to a similar valence-rearranging constraint: Any objects subcategorized by the verb are removed from ARG-ST and replaced with an NP of the form *X's way* and a locative expression, as formalized in Sag (2012, 142). Hence, even ditransitive verbs are stripped of their complements by the *Way* Construction, as in (i). We would in addition type the original object frame elements as *ini-index*, ensuring their INI interpretation. Further extensions will be needed to accommodate the fact that Sag's analysis does not consider a frequently noted semantic distinction between subspecies of the *Way* Construction, depending on whether the verb denotes a manner of movement (often metaphorical) along some path, *whistled her way along the shore*, versus the means by which movement (also often metaphorical) toward some goal or outcome is achieved, *pushed his way to the edge* (Goldberg, 1995; Jackendoff, 1990; Levin & Rappaport Hovav, 1988.

i.   @The depths of American political corruption became glaringly apparent when DeVos admitted that she donated ∅ her way into her job.

(51) is responsible for resolving the values of VAL and GAP, given the content of ARG-ST.

An example of a short passive is depicted in Figure 14. Here, the PP in ARG-ST is resolved as a *covert-sign* with a *ini-index* and therefore it is missing from VAL and GAP. Had the PP been resolved as *overt-sign*, then its index would be *ref-index* and the PP would have been overtly realized as a complement of *feed*.[30]

Note that in our analysis, the implicit agent of the short passive is still a member of ARG-ST, which predicts that it should be visible to binding theory as in (84).

(84)   a. [@]The first "email" was sent by Ray Tomlinson in 1971. He chose the @ sign to separate the local part from the domain. The first email address was "tomlinson@bbntenexa" and the email was sent to himself.

   b. [@]The very first email was sent by computer engineer Ray Tomlinson on July 1st 1971. The message probably consisted of only a few words and letters and was sent to himself, but the implications would change communications worldwide forever.

   c. [@]In a newly declassified email that Susan Rice sent to herself on January 20, 2017, the former national-security adviser said that …Rice's email was sent to herself 15 days after the Oval Office meeting.

---

[30] The passive construction in (83) overgenerates, since it wrongly predicts as good sentences like the one in (i). Sag (2012, 131) proposes to define the mutually exclusive types *pseudo-transitive-verb* and *transitive-verb* to model the behavior of verbs like *weigh* in (i) and (ii), respectively, adding the caveat, "refinements are of course possible."

   i. *357 pounds is weighed by Trump.
   ii. Trump is weighed frequently by Dr. Ronnie.

The envisioned refinements would seemingly involve evidence – probably semantic, but conceivably syntactic as well – to independently motivate the pseudo-transitive versus transitive type distinction in verb lexemes. Caution, however, might dictate awaiting the arrival of this evidence before formalizing the type distinction because there may be valid approaches that do not require the postulation of two types. For example, it would be possible to simply omit the "pseudo-passive" verbs from the domain of the morphological function f_{pass} that outputs passive participles (i.e. f_{pass} could take the phonology and the LID value of the stem, in order to distinguish passivizable stems from their homophonous counterparts that lack a passive form). Such an approach would formalize the intuition that the so-called pseudo-transitive verbs are an unsystematic collection of often idiosyncratic exceptions to an otherwise general rule, perhaps with an eye to phenomena like the (near?) unique existence of a verb, *rumored*, which has no forms other than passive participle. Exceptions are sometimes just that. A first step to answering the question whether there is more structure to the phenomena than we have so far discovered might entail obtaining a list of all the (English) verb lexemes that have at least two arguments and don't have a passive participle form in order to examine what they might have in common. We leave that task to future research.

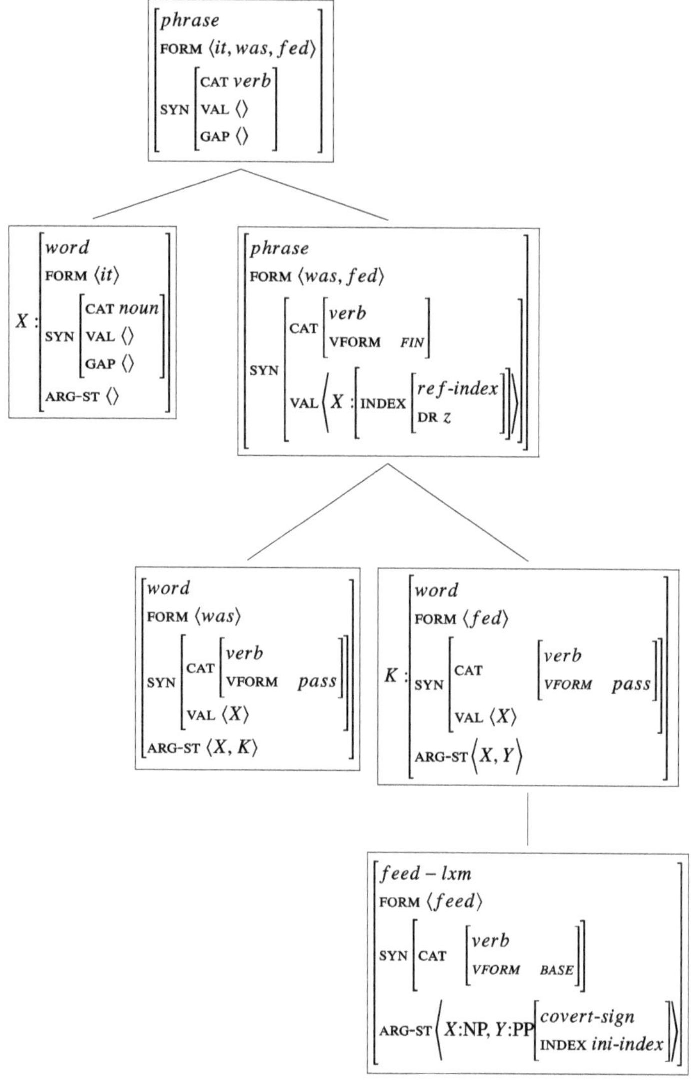

Figure 14 Short passive clause *It was fed* (abbreviated).

d. @(...) a settlement had been executed by Miss Bolton as soon as she came of age, by which an absolute general power of appointment was given to herself and her proposed husband jointly in priority to the other trustees of the settlement.

Our account also predicts that an implicit passive agent can control secondary predicates, as we noted in Section 2.3, with examples like (85a,b) or pro subjects of infinitives as in (85c). Lexically licensed NI – for example, of active-voice objects, can equally control secondary predicates, as in (85b). In our analysis, such NI arguments are still members of ARG-ST, and therefore are visible to the independently motivated valence-extending constructions that license such control structures.

(85)　a. @The game was played barefoot.

　　　b. @The first football match the Nigerian football team played!! They played barefoot and won the match 5–0.

　　　c.　The boat was sunk to collect the insurance.
　　　　 (Jackendoff, 1987, 408)

3.6　Semantics of NI

We now turn to how discourse referents associated with INI and DNI indices are interpreted. One possibility would be to add a definite quantifier to the semantic representation of DNI arguments and an indefinite to that of INI arguments, which could be done by modifying the constructions discussed so far, or via closure rules. However, we believe that adding quantifiers would make the wrong predictions. For example, if INI signs were bound by an existential quantifier, then such quantifier would be expected to give rise to scope ambiguities, all else being equal, but this prediction is not borne out.

Consider the examples in (86), which contain no implicit arguments. As expected, two readings of the indefinite NP "a check of $100" arise depending on whether it receives wide or narrow scope.

(86)　a.　I didn't contribute a check$_x$ of $100 to the Red Cross. That$_x$ was a gift from someone else. I gave a 5 dollar bill.
　　　　　(Wide scope: $\exists x(check(x,\$100) \wedge \neg contribute(I,x))$)

　　　b.　I didn't contribute a check$_x$ of $100 to the Red Cross. In fact, I've never made any contributions, ever.
　　　　　(Narrow scope: $\neg\exists x(check(x,\$100) \wedge contribute(I,x))$)

However, only the narrow scope reading is possible if the theme is INI instead, as (87) illustrates, a an observation originally due to Condoravdi and Gawron (1996, 3).

(87)　　I didn't contribute ∅ to the Red Cross.
　　　　(= I didn't contribute anything to the Red Cross)

Like its overt counterparts in (86), the INI theme is usually anaphorically accessible to discourse continuations, as in (88a). But as expected, such anaphora are not possible in the presence of negation precisely because the INI theme must reside under its scope, as (88b) shows.[31] Thus, the continuation in (88b) has no antecedent to bind to.

(88) a.   I contributed $\emptyset_x$ to the Red Cross. It$_x$ was a rather large sum.

  b.   I didn't contribute $\emptyset_x$ to the Red Cross. #It$_x$ was a rather large sum.

Attested examples of NI anaphoric dependencies are provided in (89).

(89) a.   The children began to sing $\emptyset_x$. It$_x$ was the song Henryk Bley had composed with them before they went.
       [COCA 1990 FIC]

  b. @[The] young lady reminded us they close at 4 so we ate $\emptyset_x$ quickly and it$_x$ was good but a little overpriced.

  c.   Thirteen said, "you gotta give people food, you know? I mean, to be peaceable." Behind him, Smokey, plate just under her chin, ate $\emptyset_x$ eagerly. It$_x$ had meat in it too. (Delany, *Dhalgren*, 138)

Incidentally, anaphora can target INI passive agents as well, as evidenced by (90). See Koenig and Mauner (1999, 216) and Mauner and Koenig (2000) for arguments that such dependencies are instances of bridging (Clark, 1975; Erkü & Gundel, 1987; Hawkins, 1978; Prince, 1981b).

(90) a. @The first time I was ghosted $\emptyset_x$ he$_x$ came back 3 months later...

  b. @You won't believe this but I have witnesses. When I was carjacked $\emptyset_x$ he$_x$ hopped into my passenger seat and set the gun on his lap...

  c. @I'm so sorry that happened friend. When I was assaulted $\emptyset_x$, he$_x$ drugged me first...

  d. @I got married $\emptyset_x$, she$_x$ cheated on me, and she's pregnant by someone else!

Given these observations, we conclude that NI arguments are not associated with any quantifier in logical form. In our account, the variables associated

---

[31] Examples like (i–ii) appear to challenge the claim that scope-embedded INI arguments cannot be bound anaphorically. However, these are instances of an independent phenomenon known as modal/quanfiticational subordination, first noted by Roberts (1987), in which introduction of a modal allows indefinite NPs that have narrow scope readings to escape the interpretive effect of the negation and consequently be anaphorically bound to across clauses.

   i. This time, I didn't contribute $\emptyset_x$ to the Red Cross. Anyway, it$_x$ wouldn't have been much.
   ii. I didn't contribute $\emptyset_x$ this year because of the embezzlement scandal. It$_x$ was going to be $1,000!

with indices typed *ini-index* are directly interpreted as existential indefinites, and variables associated with indices typed as *dni-index* are directly interpreted as definites. Following Farkas and de Swart (2003, ch. 3) we assume that such direct interpretations are enforced model-theoretically: When the semantic representation is interpreted against a model, the variables that are associated with *ini-index* and *dni-index* are interpreted as if they had a quantifier. The truth-conditional interpretation for n-ary predicate P is traditionally formalized as $[\![P(x_1,...,x_i)]\!] = 1$ *iff* $\langle [\![x_1]\!], ..., [\![x_n]\!] \rangle \in F(P)$, where F is the interpretation function. We adopt this approach to the interpretation of our semantic frames as seen in (91). By *P-fr* we mean a variable over FRAME predicate types.

$$(91) \quad \left[\!\!\left[\begin{matrix} P\text{-}fr \\ \text{SIT} \quad S \\ \text{FES} \quad \langle X_1,...,X_n \rangle \end{matrix} \right]\!\!\right] = 1 \;\; \textit{iff} \;\; \langle [\![S]\!], [\![X_1]\!], ..., [\![X_n]\!] \rangle \in F(P\text{-}fr)$$

The interpretation of *ref-index* and *pro-index* indices is straightforward: For all $X_{1..n}$ indices, the value of their respective discourse markers is determined by the valuation function $val()$ as shown in (92).

$$(92) \quad \text{a.} \quad \left[\!\!\left[\begin{matrix} ref\text{-}index \\ \text{DR} \quad v \end{matrix} \right]\!\!\right] = val(v)$$

$$\text{b.} \quad \left[\!\!\left[\begin{matrix} pro\text{-}index \\ \text{DR} \quad v \end{matrix} \right]\!\!\right] = val(v)$$

In order for $val(v)$ to be defined, the variable v has to already have been bound to a quantifier or to an equality. Otherwise, $val(v)$ is undefined and the value of v has no interpretation, as usual in certain semantic theories like Groenendijk and Stokhof (1991), Kamp and Reyle (1993), and Kamp and van Eijck (1997). Thus, the discourse markers of *ref-index* and *pro-index* signs are free, and cannot be interpreted with $val()$. Farkas and de Swart (2003, ch. 3) propose to solve the problem of defining the truth-conditions of predicates with implicit arguments by allowing the denotation of the predicate to determine the value of its free variables. We do the same, but in addition introduce constraints that account for the differences between DNI and INI.

We augment (92) with two extra cases, drawing from Gundel, Hedberg, and Zacharski's (1993) implicational givenness hierarchy for NPs. We assume that an entity e that is the value of a DNI variable must be a uniquely identifiable member of the Dom(ain) in the given context, as shown in (93a). A uniquely identifiable referent is an entity that is in the set of given entities and that has core characteristics which are not shared by any other entity that is also given.

This uniquely identifiable constraint is independently needed to license the use of definite descriptions (Gundel et al., 1993).

(93)
  a. $\left[\!\left[\begin{bmatrix} dni\text{-}index \\ \text{DR} \quad v \end{bmatrix}\right]\!\right] = e \; iff \; \exists e(e \in Dom \wedge \text{Uniquely Identifiable}(e) \wedge val(v) = e)$

  b. $\left[\!\left[\begin{bmatrix} ini\text{-}index \\ \text{DR} \quad v \end{bmatrix}\right]\!\right] = e \; iff \; \exists e(e \in Dom \wedge \text{Type-Identifiable}(e) \wedge val(v) = e)$

The variables of NI indices implicitly evoke a quantificational interpretation as in (93). Thus, for NI variables, their value is some entity from Dom.[32] In this analysis *dni-index* referents have uniquely identifying properties in the given context, just like those referents that are characterizable with the definite determiner *the*. Analogously, the entity *e* in (92b) must be type-identifiable, rather than uniquely identifiable. Thus, *ini-index* referents are not assumed to be known by the addressee, just like those referents that are characterizable with indefinite determiner *a(n)*.

As in Gundel et al.'s (1993) account of definite and indefinite determiners, the interpretation of DNI and INI variables depends on their cognitive status, not logical form. The entity that is identified according to Gundel et al.'s concept of *unique identifiability* is without mystery; the Domain is a set of individuals and the entity identified is a member of that set. The concept of TYPE IDENTIFIABILITY is less straightforward. Although providing several helpful illustrative examples, the only abstract statement of the concept provided is "TYPE IDENTIFIABLE: The addressee is able to access a representation of the type of object described by the expression" (Gundel et al., 1993, 276). We interpret the "type of object" notion set-theoretically as shown in (94).

(94)   An individual *i* in domain Dom is type-identifiable in utterance *u* iff an auditor of *u* can ascertain in context a proper subset of Dom of which *i* is a member.

The construal of implicit arguments as prototypical participants, and their failure to behave like regular quantified arguments thus follows from their status. Once an NI variable is assigned a value by the *val()* function, it may be anaphorically bound, as in (89). It has become salient in the speaker's mental representation. See Farkas and de Swart (2003, ch. 3) for a unification-based

---

[32] The contextual constraint imposed in (93a) may be presuppositional in nature, and if so, we could assume that it is embedded under Beaver's (1992) ∂-operator, following the analysis of definite descriptions in Coppock and Beaver (2015).

mechanism for binding to implicit arguments that is fully compatible with the present account, and see also Condoravdi and Gawron (1996) for a related analysis of the interpretation of implicit locative anaphora.

4 Conclusion

This Element recognizes two kinds of mismatch between the predicator's arguments and the overt constituents that realize those arguments. On the one hand, we have implicit arguments that derive part of their semantic value from elsewhere in the linguistic representation, as exemplified by covert arguments bound by a quantifier (including generic "*pro*"), imperative subjects, and controlled subjects. On the other, we have implicit arguments whose semantics is determined directly from context, independently of anything else in the logical form of the sentence. The latter group, which constitutes our principal concern, falls under what Fillmore (1986) termed null instantiation (NI). We retain this terminology as well as recognizing Fillmore's two main (and in our view exhaustive) subtypes: definite NI and indefinite NI, which we ground on the givenness hierarchy outlined by Gundel et al. (1993), as a cognitive level equivalent to definite and indefinite quantification.

Drawing from Ruppenhofer and Michaelis (2010; 2014), we also make a distinction that cuts across the indefinite/definite null instantiation division. What we have termed lexically licensed NI is a property of the individual listeme ("off-the-shelf" lexical entry), which is most readily appreciated in the observation that verbs with very similar meanings frequently display different NI potentials. Lexically licensed NI was the exclusive concern of Fillmore's original NI paper (Fillmore, 1986). The contrasting type of NI is characterized by constructions that endow an argument with NI potential not present in the lexical entry, which we refer to as contextually licensed NI because the constructions involved are dependent in part on properties of the discourse context. We formulate this account in SBCG, which we find well suited to explicitly characterize lexical and constructional patterns and idiosyncrasies, as well as their syntactic, semantic, and pragmatic interactions with the overall grammar. A welcome result of this research would be for it to stimulate comparable investigations in languages other than English.

References

Ariel, M. (2001). Accessibility theory: An overview. In T. Sanders, J. Schilperoord, & W. Spooren (Eds.), *Text representation: Linguistic and psycholinguistic aspects* (Vol. 8, pp. 29–87). Amsterdam: John Benjamins.

Beaver, D. (1992). The kinematics of presupposition. In P. Dekker & M. Stokhof (Eds.), *Proceedings of the Eighth Amsterdam Colloquium* (pp. 17–36). Amsterdam: Institute of Logic, Language and Computation.

Bender, E. (1999). Constituting context: Null objects in English recipes revisited. In J. Alexander, N.- R. Han, & M. M. Fox (Eds.), *Proceedings of the 23rd Annual Penn Linguistics Colloquium* (Vol. 6, pp. 53–68). Retrieved from www.ling.upenn.edu/papers/pwpl/v6.1/bender.ps.

Bender, E., & Kathol, A. (2001). Constructional effects of just because ... doesn't mean ... In *Proceedings of the annual meeting of the Berkeley Linguistics Society, (27)*1.

Bhatt, R., & Pancheva, R. (2006). Implicit arguments. In *The Wiley Blackwell companion to syntax, second edition* (pp. 558–588). Oxford: Blackwell.

Boeckx, C. (1998). A minimalist view of the passive. In *MIT working papers in linguistics.* Cambridge, MA: MIT Press.

Boneh, N. (2019). Dispositions and characterizing sentences. *Glossa: A Journal of General Linguistics, 4*(1), 130.

Bresnan, J. (2001). *Lexical-functional syntax*. Oxford: Blackwell.

Bresnan, J., & Zaenen, A. (1990). Deep unaccusativity in LFG. In K. Dziwirek, P. Farrell, & E. Mejías-Bikandi (Eds.), *Grammatical relations: A cross-theoretical perspective* (pp. 45–57). Stanford, CA: Stanford University.

Brisson, C. (1994). The licensing of unexpressed objects in English verbs. In *Proceedings of the 30th annual meeting of the Chicago Linguistic Society* (Vol. 30, pp. 90–102). Chicago, IL: Chicago Linguistic Society.

Chomsky, N. (1986). *Knowledge of language: Its nature, origin, and use*. New York: Praeger.

Clark, H. H. (1975). Bridging. In *Proceedings of the Conference on Theoretical Issues in Natural Language Processing* (pp. 169–174). Cambridge, MA: Association for Computational Linguistics.

Condoravdi, C., & Gawron, J. M. (1996). The context-dependency of implicit arguments. In M. Kanazawa, C. Piñón, & H. E. de Swart (Eds.), *Quantifiers, deduction and context* (pp. 1–32). Stanford, CA: CSLI.

Coppock, E., & Beaver, D. (2015). Definiteness and determinacy. *Linguistics and Philosophy, 38*(5), 377–435.

Cornish, F. (2007). Implicit internal arguments, event structure, predication and anaphoric reference. In N. Hedberg & R. Zacharski (Eds.), *The grammar–pragmatics interface: Essays in honor of Jeanette K. Gundel* (pp. 189–216). Amsterdam: John Benjamins.

Crichton, M. (2002). *Prey*. New York: Avon Books.

Culicover, P. W., & Jackendoff, R. (2005). *Simpler syntax*. Oxford: Oxford University Press.

David, O. A. (2016). Metaphor in the grammar of argument realization (Unpublished doctoral dissertation). University of California, Berkeley.

Davis, A. (2001). *Linking by types in the hierarchical lexicon*. Stanford, CA: CSLI.

Davis, A., Koenig, J.- P., & Wechsler, S. (2021). Argument structure and linking. In S. Müller, A. Abeillé, R. D. Borsley, & J.- P. Koenig (Eds.), *Head Driven Phrase Structure Grammar* (pp. 336–390). Berlin: Language Science Press.

Delany, Samuel R. (1975). *Dhalgren*. New York: Bantam Books.

Dowty, D. R. (1985). On recent analyses of the semantics of control. *Linguistics and Philosophy, 8*(3), 291–331.

Erkü, F., & Gundel, J. K. (1987). The pragmatics of indirect anaphors. In J. Verschueren & M. Bertuccelli-Papi (Eds.), *The pragmatic perspective: Selected papers from the 1985 International Pragmatics Conference* (pp. 533–545). Amsterdam: John Benjamins.

Farkas, D. F., & de Swart, H. E. (2003). *The semantics of incorporation: From argument structure to discourse transparency*. Stanford, CA: CSLI.

Fillmore, C. J. (1969). Types of lexical information. In K. Ferenc (Ed.), *Studies in syntax and semantics* (Vol. 12, pp. 109–137). Dordrecht: Reidel.

Fillmore, C. J. (1986). Pragmatically controlled zero anaphora. In *Annual meeting of the Berkeley Linguistics Society* (Vol. 12, pp. 95–107). Berkeley, CA: Berkeley Linguistics Society.

Fillmore, C. J. (1988). The mechanisms of "construction grammar." In *Annual meeting of the Berkeley Linguistics Society* (Vol. 14, pp. 35–55). Berkeley, CA: Berkeley Linguistics Society.

Fillmore, C. J. (2013). Berkeley Construction Grammar. In T. Hoffman & G. Trousdale (Eds.), *The Oxford handbook of linguistic analysis* (pp. 111–132). Oxford: Oxford University Press.

Fillmore, C. J., Johnson, C. R., & Petruck, M. R. (2003). Background to FrameNet. *International Journal of Lexicography, 16*(3), 235–250.

Flickinger, D. P. (1987). Lexical rules in the hierarchical lexicon (Unpublished doctoral dissertation). Stanford University.

Flowers, A. J. (2018). *Valkyrie Uprising*.

Fodor, J. A., & Fodor, J. D. (1980). Functional structure, quantifiers, and meaning postulates. *Linguistic Inquiry, 11*(4), 759–770.

Gillon, B. (2012). Implicit complements: A dilemma for model theoretic semantics. *Linguistics and Philosophy, 35*(4), 313–359.

Ginzburg, J., & Sag, I. A. (2000). *Interrogative investigations: The form, meaning and use of English interrogative constructions*. Stanford, CA: CSLI.

Glass, L. (2021). English verbs can omit their objects when they describe routines. *English Language and Linguistics, 26*(1): 49–73.

Goldberg, A. E. (1995). *Constructions: A construction grammar approach to argument structure*. Chicago, IL: University of Chicago Press.

Goldberg, A. E. (2006). *Constructions at work: The nature of generalization in language*. Oxford: Oxford University Press.

Goldberg, A. E. (2019). *Explain me this: Creativity, competition and the partial productivity of constructions*. Princeton, NJ: Princeton University Press.

Gregory, M. L., & Michaelis, L. A. (2001). Topicalization and left dislocation: A functional opposition revisited. *Journal of Pragmatics, 33*, 1665–1706.

Grimshaw, J. (1990). *Argument structure*. Cambridge, MA: MIT Press.

Groenendijk, J., & Stokhof, M. (1991). Dynamic predicate logic. *Linguistics and Philosophy, 14*(1), 39–100.

Gundel, J. K., Hedberg, N., & Zacharski, R. (1993). Cognitive status and the form of referring expressions in discourse. *Language, 69*(2), 274–307.

Haegeman, L., & Ihsane, T. (2001). Adult null subjects in the non-pro-drop languages: Two diary dialects. *Language Acquisition, 9*(4), 329–346.

Hawkins, J. (1978). *Definiteness and indefiniteness: A study in reference and grammaticality prediction*. Atlantic Highlands, NJ: Humanities Press.

Heider, P. M. (2005). The semantics of optionality (PhD dissertation). University at Buffalo.

Horn, L. (1984). Toward a new taxonomy for pragmatic inference: Q-based and r-based implicature. In D. Schiffrin (Ed.), *Meaning, form, and use in context: Linguistic applications* (pp. 11–42). Washington, DC: Georgetown University Press.

Huddleston, R. D., & Pullum, G. K. (2002). *The Cambridge grammar of the English language*. Cambridge: Cambridge University Press.

Iordăchioaia, G., & Richter, F. (2015). Negative concord with polyadic quantifiers: The case of Romanian. *Natural Language and Linguistic Theory, 33*(2), 607–658.

Jackendoff, R. (1987). The status of thematic relations in linguistic theory. *Linguistic Inquiry, 18*(3), 369–411.

Jackendoff, R. (1990). *Semantic structures*. Cambridge, MA: MIT Press.

Kamp, H., & Reyle, U. (1993). *From discourse to logic: An introduction to modeltheoretic semantics of natural language, formal logic and DRT.* Dordrecht: Kluwer.

Kamp, H., & van Eijck, J. (1997). Representing discourse in context. In J. van Benthem & A. ter Meulen (Eds.), *Handbook of logic, language and information* (pp. 243–258). Amsterdam: Elsevier Science.

Kathol, A. (2001). Non-existence of parasitic gaps in German. In P. W. Culicover & P. M. Postal (Eds.), *In parasitic gaps* (pp. 315–338). Cambridge, MA: MIT Press.

Kay, P. (2002). English subjectless tagged sentences. *Language, 78*(3), 453–481.

Kay, P. (2004). Null complementation constructions. (Unpublished manuscript, University of California, Berkeley).

Kay, P., & Fillmore, C. J. (1999). Grammatical constructions and linguistic generalizations: The *what's x doing y?* construction. *Language, 75*(1), 1–33.

Keenan, E., & Comrie, B. (1977). Noun phrase accessibility and universal grammar. *Linguistic Inquiry, 8*(1), 63–99.

Koenig, J.- P. (1999). *Lexical relations.* Stanford, CA: Stanford University Press.

Koenig, J.- P., & Davis, A. (2003). Semantically transparent linking in HPSG. In S. Müller (Ed.), *Proceedings of the HPSG-2003 conference, Michigan State University, East Lansing* (pp. 222–235). Stanford, CA: CSLI Publications.

Koenig, J.- P., & Davis, A. (2006). The key to lexical semantic representations. *Journal of Linguistics, 42*, 71–108.

Koenig, J.- P., & Mauner, G. (1999). A-definites and the discourse status of implicit arguments. *Journal of Semantics, 16*(3), 207–236.

Lambrecht, K., & Lemoine, K. (2005). Definite null objects in (spoken) French: A construction grammar account. In H. C. Boas & M. Fried (Eds.), *Grammatical constructions: Back to the roots* (pp. 157–199). Amsterdam: John Benjamins.

L'Amour, L. (2001) *May there be a road.* New York: Bantam Books.

Landau, I. (2010). The explicit syntax of implicit arguments. *Linguistic Inquiry, 41*(3), 357–388.

Levin, B. (1993). *English verb classes and alternations: A preliminary investigation.* Chicago, IL: University of Chicago Press.

Levin, B., & Rappaport Hovav, M. (1988). Lexical subordination. In *Proceedings of the general session at the 24th regional meeting of the Chicago Linguistics Society* (Vol. 24–1, pp. 275–289).

Levin, B., & Rappaport Hovav, M. (2005). *Argument realization*. Cambridge: Cambridge University Press.

Levin, L. S. (1985). *Operations on lexical forms: unaccusative rules in germanic languages* (PhD thesis). MIT.

Levine, R. D., & Hukari, T. E. (2006). *The unity of unbounded dependency constructions*. Stanford, CA: CSLI Publications.

Lyngfeld, B. (2012). Re-thinking FNI: On null instantiation and control in construction grammar. *Constructions and Frames*, *4*(1), 1–23.

Mauner, G., & Koenig, J.- P. (2000). Linguistic vs. conceptual sources of implicit agents in sentence comprehension. *Journal of Memory and Language*, *43*(1), 110–134.

McCawley, J. D. (1968). The role of semantics in a grammar. In E. Bach & R. T. Harms (Eds.), *Universals of linguistic theory* (pp. 124–169). New York: Holt, Reinhart, and Winston.

Michaelis, L. (2003). Headless constructions and coercion by construction. In E. J. Francis & L. A. Michaelis (Eds.), *Mismatch: Form–function incongruity and the architecture of grammar* (pp. 259–310). Stanford, CA: CSLI Publications.

Michaelis, L. (2012). Making the case for construction grammar. In H. Boas & I. A. Sag (Eds.), *Sign-Based Construction Grammar* (pp. 31–69). Stanford, CA: CSLI Publications.

Michelioudakis, D. (2021). Rethinking implicit agents: Syntax cares but not always. In A. Bárány, T. Biberauer, J. Douglas, & S. Vikner (Eds.), *Syntactic architecture and its consequences III: Inside syntax* (pp. 287–311). Berlin: Language Science Press.

Miller, P. H., & Monachesi, P. (2003). Les pronoms clitiques dans les langues romanes. In D. Godard (Ed.), *Les langues romanes, problèmes de la phrase simple* (pp. 53–106). Paris: Editions du CNRS. (Translated into English: Clitic pronouns in the Romance langagues. In D. Godard (Ed.), *The Romance languages*, Stanford, CA: CSLI Publications).

Mittwoch, A. (2005). Unspecified arguments in episodic and habitual sentences. In N. Erteschik-Shir & T. Rapoport (Eds.), *The syntax of aspect: Deriving thematic and aspectual interpretation* (pp. 237–254). Oxford: Oxford University Press.

Müller, S. (2008). Depictive secondary predicates in German and English. In C. Schroeder, G. Hentschel, & W. Boeder (Eds.), *Secondary predicates in Eastern European languages and beyond* (pp. 255–273). Oldenburg: BIS-Verlag. Retrieved from https://hpsg.hu-berlin.de/~stefan/Pub/depiktiv-2006.html.

O'Gorman, T. J. (2019). Bringing together computational and linguistic models of implicit role interpretation (Unpublished doctoral dissertation). University of Colorado at Boulder.

Pollard, C., & Sag, I. A. (1994). *Head-Driven Phrase Structure Grammar*. Chicago, IL: University of Chicago Press.

Prince, E. F. (1981a). Topicalization, focus-movement, and Yiddish-movement: A pragmatic differentiation. In *The proceedings of the seventh annual meeting of the Berkeley Linguistics Society* (pp. 249–264). Berkeley, CA: Berkeley Linguistics Society.

Prince, E. F. (1981b). Towards a taxonomy of given-new information. In P. Cole (Ed.), *Radical pragmatics* (pp. 223–255). New York: Academic Press.

Rappaport Hovav, M., & Levin, B. (1998). Building verb meanings. In M. Butt & W. Geuder (Eds.), *The projection of arguments: Lexical and compositional factors* (pp. 97–134). Stanford, CA: Center for the Study of Language and Information.

Reape, M. (1996). Getting things in order. In H. Bunt & A. van Horck (Eds.), *Discontinuous constituency* (pp. 209–253). Berlin: Mouton de Gruyter.

Reinöhl, U., & Ellison, T. M. (2024). Metaphor forces argument overtness. *Linguistics*, *62*(2), 795–847.

Resnik, P. (1993). Selection and information: A class-based approach to lexical relationships (PhD dissertation). University of Pennsylvania.

Resnik, P. (1996). Selectional constraints: An information-theoretic model and its computational realization. *Cognition*, *61*(1–2), 127–159.

Rice, S. (1988). Unlikely lexical entries. In *Annual meeting of the Berkeley Linguistics Society* (Vol. 14, pp. 202–212). Berkeley, CA: Berkeley Linguistics Society.

Rizzi, L. (1986). Null objects in italian and the theory of pro. *Linguistic Inquiry*, *17*(3), 501–557.

Roberts, C. (1987). Modal subordination, anaphora and distributivity. PhD. thesis, University of Massachusetts at Amherst.

Ruppenhofer, J. (2004). The interaction of valence and information structure (PhD thesis). University of California, Berkeley.

Ruppenhofer, J., & Michaelis, L. A. (2010). A constructional account of genre-based argument omissions. In *Constructions and frames* (Vol. 2, pp. 158–184). Amsterdam: John Benjamins.

Ruppenhofer, J., & Michaelis, L. A. (2014). Frames and the interpretation of omitted arguments in English. In S. K. Bourns & L. Myers (Eds.), *Linguistic perspectives on structure and context: Studies in honor of Knud Lambrecht* (pp. 57–86). Amsterdam: John Benjamins.

Sag, I. A. (1997). English relative clause constructions. *Journal of Linguistics, 33*(2), 431–484.

Sag, I. A. (2010). English filler-gap constructions. *Language, 86*(3), 486–545.

Sag, I. A. (2012). Sign-based construction grammar: An informal synopsis. In H. Boas & I. A. Sag (Eds.), *Sign-based construction grammar* (pp. 69 – 202). Stanford, CA: CSLI Publications.

Sag, I. A., Chaves, R. P., Abeillé, A., Estigarribia, B., Flickinger, D., Kay, P., …Wasow, T. (2020). Lessons from the English auxiliary system. *Journal of Linguistics, 56*(1), p. 69.

Sag, I. A., Wasow, T., & Bender, E. M. (2003). *Syntactic theory: A formal introduction.* 2nd edition. Stanford, CA: CSLI Publications.

Shopen, T. (1973). Ellipsis as grammatical indeterminacy. *Foundations of Language, 10*, 65–77.

Stein, S. (1958) *Second-class taxi.* Cape Town: Africasouth Paperbacks.

Stine, R. L. (undated). *Camp Fear Ghouls.* New York: Simon & Schuster [pages unnumbered].

Wechsler, S., & Zlatic, L. (2003). *The many faces of agreement: Morphology, syntax, semantics, and discourse factors in Serbo-Croatian agreement.* Stanford, CA: CSLI Publications.

Construction Grammar

Thomas Hoffmann
Catholic University of Eichstätt-Ingolstadt

Thomas Hoffmann is Full Professor and Chair of English Language and Linguistics at the Catholic University of Eichstätt-Ingolstadt. His main research interests are usage-based Construction Grammar, language variation and change and linguistic creativity. He has published widely in international journals such as *Cognitive Linguistics, English Language and Linguistics*, and *English World-Wide*. His monographs *Preposition Placement in English* (2011) and *English Comparative Correlatives: Diachronic and Synchronic Variation at the Lexicon-Syntax Interface* (2019) were both published by Cambridge University Press. His textbook on *Construction Grammar: The Structure of English* (2022) as well as an Element on *The Cognitive Foundation of Post-colonial Englishes: Construction Grammar as the Cognitive Theory for the Dynamic Model* (2021) have also both been published with Cambridge University Press. He is also co-editor (with Graeme Trousdale) of *The Oxford Handbook of Construction Grammar* (2013, Oxford University Press).

Alexander Bergs
Osnabrück University

Alexander Bergs joined the Institute for English and American Studies at Osnabrück University, Germany, in 2006 when he became Full Professor and Chair of English Language and Linguistics. His research interests include, among others, language variation and change, constructional approaches to language, the role of context in language, the syntax/pragmatics interface, and cognitive poetics. His works include several authored and edited books (*Social Networks and Historical Sociolinguistics, Modern Scots, Contexts and Constructions, Constructions and Language Change*), a short textbook on *Synchronic English Linguistics*, one on *Understanding Language Change* (with Kate Burridge) and the two-volume *Handbook of English Historical Linguistics* (ed. with Laurel Brinton; now available as five-volume paperback) as well as more than fifty papers in high-profile international journals and edited volumes. Alexander Bergs has taught at the Universities of Düsseldorf, Bonn, Santiago de Compostela, Wisconsin-Milwaukee, Catania, Vigo, Thessaloniki, Athens, and Dalian and has organized numerous international workshops and conferences.

About the Series

Construction Grammar is the leading cognitive theory of syntax. The present Elements series will survey its theoretical building blocks, show how Construction Grammar can capture various linguistic phenomena across a wide range of typologically different languages, and identify emerging frontier topics from a theoretical, empirical and applied perspective.

For EU product safety concerns, contact us at Calle de José Abascal, 56–1°,
28003 Madrid, Spain or eugpsr@cambridge.org.

www.ingramcontent.com/pod-product-compliance
Ingram Content Group UK Ltd.
Pitfield, Milton Keynes, MK11 3LW, UK
UKHW020327040925
462578UK00021B/462